15 MINUTE
FRENCH
LEARN IN JUST 12 WEEKS

Caroline Lemoine

DK | Penguin
Random
House

Senior Editors Angeles Gavira, Christine Stroyan
Project Art Editor Vanessa Marr
DTP Designer John Goldsmid
Jacket Design Development Manager Sophia MTT
Jacket Designer Juhi Sheth
Pre-Producer David Almond
Senior Producer Ana Vallarino
Associate Publisher Liz Wheeler
Publishing Director Jonathan Metcalf

**Language content for Dorling Kindersley by
g-and-w publishing.**

**Produced for Dorling Kindersley by
Schermuly Design Co.**

First published in Great Britain in 2005.
This revised edition published in 2018 by
Dorling Kindersley Limited
80 Strand, London WC2R 0RL.

Copyright © 2005, 2012, 2018 Dorling Kindersley Limited
A Penguin Random House Company

2 4 6 8 10 9 7 5 3 1
01-305997-Jan/2018

A CIP catalogue record is available for this book
from the British Library.
ISBN 978-0-2413-0222-4

Printed in China

A WORLD OF IDEAS:
SEE ALL THERE IS TO KNOW

www.dk.com

CONTENTS

How to use this book

The main part of the book is devoted to 12 themed chapters, broken down into five 15-minute daily lessons, the last of which is a revision lesson. So, in just 12 weeks you will have completed the course. A concluding reference section contains a menu guide and English-to-French and French-to-English dictionaries.

Warm up
Each day starts with a warm up that encourages you to recall vocabulary or phrases you have learned previously. To the right of the heading bar you will see how long you need to spend on each exercise.

Instructions
Each exercise is numbered and introduced by instructions that explain what to do. In some cases additional information is given about the language point being covered.

Cultural/Conversational tip
These panels provide additional insights into life in France and language usage.

How to use the flap
The book's cover flaps allow you to conceal the French so that you can test whether you have remembered correctly.

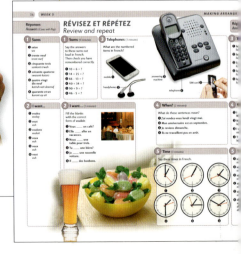

Revision pages
A recap of selected elements of previous lessons helps to reinforce your knowledge.

4 Useful phrases (5 minutes)

Learn these phrases. Read the English under the pictures and say the phrase in French as shown on the right. Then conceal the French with the cover flap and test yourself.

Je voudrais un grand café, s'il vous plaît.
juh voodray uñ groñ kafay, seel voo play

I'd like a large black coffee, please.

C'est tout?
say too

Is that all?

Je prends un croissant.
juh proñ uñ krossoñ

I'll have a croissant.

C'est combien?
say koñbyañ

How much is that?

le pain
luh pañ
bread

le café au lait
luh kafay oh lay
large coffee with milk

Useful phrases
Selected phrases relevant to the topic help you speak and understand.

Oui, bien sûr.
wee, byañ syur

Yes, certainly.

Alors deux croissants. C'est combien?
alor duh krossoñ. say koñbyañ

Two croissants then. How much is that?

Quatre euros, s'il vous plaît.
katruh uroh, seel voo play

Four euros, please.

Text styles
Distinctive text styles differentiate French and English, and the pronunciation guide.

In conversation
Illustrated dialogues reflecting how vocabulary and phrases are used in everyday situations appear throughout the book.

Say it
In these exercises you are asked to apply what you have learned using different vocabulary.

6 **Say it** (2 minutes)

Do you go near the train station?

The fruit market, please.

When's the next coach to Calais?

Dictionary
A mini-dictionary provides ready reference from English to French and French to English for 2,500 words.

Menu guide
Use this guide as a reference for food terminology and popular French dishes.

Pronunciation guide

Many French sounds will already be familiar to you, but a few require special attention. Take note of how these letters are pronounced:

r   a French **r** is pronounced in the back of the throat, producing a sound a little like gargling

j   a French **j** is soft like the sound in the middle of *pleasure* (as opposed to the hard English **j** as in *major*)

n   **n** is pronounced nasally when in the combination **on, an** or **in**. Imagine saying *huh* through your nose. The nasal **n** is shown in the pronunciation with this symbol: **ñ**

ch   **ch** in French is equivalent to **sh** in English, as in *ship*

er/ez these endings are pronounced **ay** as in *play*

Pay attention also to these vowel sounds as they may vary from English:

i   as the English *keep*
au   as the English *over*
eu   as the English *fur*
oi   as the English *wag*

Below each French word or phrase you will find a pronunciation transcription. Read this, bearing in mind the tips above, and you will achieve a comprehensible result. But remember that the transcription can only ever be an approximation and that there is no real substitute for listening to and mimicking native speakers.

How to use the audio app

All the numbered exercises in each lesson, apart from the Warm ups at the beginning and the Say it exercises at the end, have recorded audio, available via a free app. The app also includes a function to record yourself and listen to yourself alongside native speakers.

To start using the audio with the book, first download the **DK 15 Minute Language Course** app on your smartphone or tablet from the App Store or Google Play. Open the app and scan the QR code on the back of this book to add it to your Library. As soon as the QR code is recognized, the audio will download.

There are two ways in which you can use the audio. The first is to read through your 15-minute lessons using the book only, and then go back and work with the audio and the book together, repeating the text in the gaps provided and then recording yourself. Or you can combine the book and the audio right from the beginning, pausing the app to read the instructions on the page as you need to. Try to say the words aloud, and practise enunciating properly. Detailed instructions on how to use the app are available from the menu bar in the app.

Remember that repetition is vital to language learning. The more often you listen to a conversation or repeat an oral exercise, the more the language will sink in.

Menu, Help/How to Use, Your Library

1 Getting started
The list of weeks will open when the audio has been downloaded. From here you can tap into each week's lessons.

When all the lessons in a week have been completed, the week button will be filled with colour and show a check mark, so you can track your progress.

2 Lessons week by week
Each numbered exercise in a lesson is listed in the app as it appears in the book. Tap on an exercise to start.

A check mark indicates when an exercise has been completed.

3 Audio for exercises
Tap the play button to hear instructions, then the exercise. You can pause the audio at any point, and return to it.

You can tap any part of the exercise to play the audio from that point.

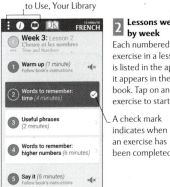

4 Record yourself
When you are in the Your recordings screen, you can record yourself reading the words or participating in the conversations with native speakers, then listen back (and rerecord if desired).

Add recording

Play recording

BONJOUR
Hello

1 **Warm up** (1 minute)

The Warm Up panel appears at the beginning of each topic. Use it to reinforce what you have already learned and to prepare yourself for moving ahead with the new subject.

In France it is part of the culture to greet family and friends with kisses on the cheek. The number of kisses varies from two to four. For example, it is usually three kisses in the south but two in Brittany. In more formal situations, a handshake is part of the normal greeting.

Salut!
saloo
Hi!

2 **Words to remember** (2 minutes)

Look at these polite expressions and say them aloud. Cover the text on the left with the cover flap and try to remember the French for each item. Check your answers.

Bonjour. *boñjoor*	Hello.
Bonsoir/bonne nuit. *boñswar/bon nwee*	Good evening/ good night.
Je m'appelle Jean. *juh mapell joñ*	My name is Jean.
Enchanté (men)/ **Enchantée** (women). *oñshontay*	Pleased to meet you.

Cultural tip The French tend to greet people with **monsieur** (*sir*), **madame** (*madam*, for older women), or **mademoiselle** (*miss*, for younger women) much more than most English-speakers would.

3 **In conversation: formal** (3 minutes)

Bonjour. Je m'appelle Céline Legrand.
boñjoor. juh mapell seleen luhgroñ

Hello. My name's Céline Legrand.

Bonjour madame. Monsieur Rossi, enchanté.
boñjoor ma-dam. musyuh rossee, oñshontay

Hello (madam). Mr Rossi, pleased to meet you.

Enchantée.
oñshontay

Pleased to meet you.

4 Put into practice (3 minutes)

Join in this conversation. Read the French beside the pictures on the left and then follow the instructions to make your reply. Then test yourself by concealing the answers on the right with the cover flap.

Bonjour monsieur.   **Bonjour mademoiselle.**
boñjoor musyuh.   *boñjoor mad-mwazel*

Hello sir.

Say: Hello mademoiselle.

Je m'appelle Martine.   **Enchanté.**
juh mapell marteen.   *oñshontay*

My name is Martine.

Say: Pleased to meet you.

5 Useful phrases (3 minutes)

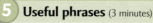

Familiarize yourself with these phrases. Read them aloud several times and try to memorize them. Conceal the French with the cover flap and test yourself.

Goodbye.	**Au revoir.** *ovwar*
See you soon.	**A bientôt.** *ah byañtoe*
See you tomorrow.	**A demain.** *ah dumañ*
Thank you (very much).	**Merci (beaucoup).** *mairsee (bohkoo)*

6 In conversation: informal (3 minutes)

Alors, à demain?
alor, ah dumañ

So, see you tomorrow?

Oui, au revoir.
wee, ovwar

Yes, goodbye.

Au revoir. A bientôt.
ovwar. ah byañtoe

Goodbye. See you soon.

1 **Warm up** (1 minute)

Say "hello" and "goodbye" in French. (pp.8–9)

Now say "My name is…" (pp.8–9)

Say "sir" and "madam". (pp.8–9)

LES RELATIONS
Relatives

In French the same word is used for relationships by marriage: **beau-père** means both father-in-law and step-father, and **belle-fille** means daughter-in-law and stepdaughter. The French for *the* is **le** or **la,** and *a* is **un** or **une**, depending on whether the word is masculine or feminine (see below).

2 **Match and repeat** (5 minutes)

Look at the people in this scene and match their numbers with the vocabulary list at the side. Read the French words aloud. Now, cover the list with the flap and test yourself.

❶ **le grand-père**
   luh groñpair

❷ **le frère**
   luh frair

❸ **la sœur**
   lah sur

❹ **le père**
   luh pair

❺ **la mère**
   lah mair

❻ **la grand-mère**
   lah groñmair

❼ **le fils**
   luh fees

❽ **la fille**
   lah feeyuh

❶ grandfather
brother ❷
❸ sister
❹ father
❺ mother
grandmother ❻   ❼ son   ❽ daughter

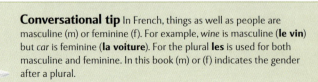

Conversational tip In French, things as well as people are masculine (m) or feminine (f). For example, *wine* is masculine (**le vin**) but *car* is feminine (**la voiture**). For the plural **les** is used for both masculine and feminine. In this book (m) or (f) indicates the gender after a plural.

3 Words to remember: relatives (4 minutes)

le mari
luh maree
husband

la femme
lah fam
wife

Nous sommes mariés.
Noo som mareeay
We are married.

Look at these words and say them aloud. Conceal the text on the right with the cover flap and try to remember the French. Check your answers. Then practise the phrases below.

sister-in-law/ stepsister	**la belle-sœur** *lah bell sur*
brother-in-law/ stepbrother	**le beau-frère** *luh boe frair*
half-sister	**la demi-sœur** *lah dumee sur*
half-brother	**le demi-frère** *luh dumee frair*
children	**les enfants** (m) *lay zoñfoñ*
I have four children.	**J'ai quatre enfants.** *jay katruh oñfoñ*
I have two stepdaughters.	**J'ai deux belles-filles.** *jay duh bell feeyuh*

4 Words to remember: numbers (3 minutes)

Memorize these words. Now cover the French and test yourself.

Be careful with the pronunciation of **deux** and **trois**. When you say them in front of a word that starts with a vowel, you need to say an extra "z" sound – for example, **deux enfants** (*two children*) is pronounced duh zoñfoñ, and **trois éclairs** (*three eclairs*), trwah zayclair. This is also true of other words.

one	**un/une** *uñ (m)/oon (f)*
two	**deux** *duh*
three	**trois** *trwah*
four	**quatre** *katruh*
five	**cinq** *sank*
six	**six** *sees*
seven	**sept** *set*
eight	**huit** *weet*
nine	**neuf** *nurf*
ten	**dix** *dees*

5 Say it (2 minutes)

I have five sons.

I have three sisters and a brother.

I have two stepsons.

MA FAMILLE
My family

1 Warm up (1 minute)

Say the French for as many members of the family as you can. (pp.10-11)

Say "I have two sons". (pp.10-11)

The French have two ways of saying *you*: **vous** for people you meet or don't know very well and **tu** for family and friends. Similarly, there are different words for *your*. The words for *my* and *your* also change depending on whether they relate to masculine, feminine, or plural nouns.

2 Words to remember (5 minutes)

Say these words out loud a few times. Cover the French with the flap and try to remember the French word for each item.

mon *moñ*	my (with masculine)
ma *mah*	my (with feminine)
mes *may*	my (with plural)
ton *toñ*	your (informal, with masculine)
ta *tah*	your (informal, with feminine)
tes *tay*	your (informal, with plural)
votre *votruh*	your (formal, with masculine or feminine)
vos *voe*	your (formal, with plural)

Voici mes parents.
vwasee may paroñ
These are my parents.

3 In conversation (4 minutes)

Vous avez des enfants?
voo zavay day zoñfoñ

Do you have any children?

Oui, j'ai deux filles.
wee, jay duh feeyuh

Yes, I have two daughters.

**Voici mes filles.
Et vous?**
*vwasee may feeyuh.
ay voo*

These are my daughters. And you?

Conversational tip The French usually ask a question by simply raising the pitch of the voice at the end of a statement - for example, **Vous voulez un café?** (*Do you want a coffee?*). You could also ask the same question by inverting the verb and subject: **Voulez-vous un café?**. Or you can put **Est-ce que** in front of the sentence **Est-ce que vous voulez un café?**

4 Useful phrases (3 minutes)

Read these phrases aloud several times and try to memorize them. Conceal the French with the cover flap and test yourself.

Do you have any brothers? (formal)	**Vous avez des frères?** *voo zavay day frair*
Do you have any brothers? (informal)	**Tu as des frères?** *tew ah day frair*

This is my husband.	**Voici mon mari.** *vwasee moñ maree*
That's my wife.	**C'est ma femme.** *say mah fam*

Is that your sister? (formal)	**C'est votre sœur?** *say votruh sur*
Is that your sister? (informal)	**C'est ta sœur?** *say tah sur*

5 Say it (2 minutes)

J'ai un beau-fils.
jay uñ boe fees

I have a stepson.

Do you have any brothers and sisters? (formal)

Do you have any children? (informal)

I have two sisters.

This is my wife.

1 **Warm up** (1 minute)

Say "See you soon".
(pp.8-9)

Say "I am married"
(pp.10-11) and
"I have a daughter".
(pp.12-13)

ETRE ET AVOIR
To be and to have

There are some essential verbs for you to learn in this course. You can use these to construct a large variety of useful phrases. The first two are **être** (*to be*) and **avoir** (*to have*). Learn them carefully as French verbs change more than English ones according to the pronoun (I, you, etc.) used.

2 **Etre: to be** (5 minutes)

Familiarize yourself with the different forms of être (*to be*). Use the cover flaps to test yourself and, when you are confident, practise the sample sentences below.

je suis *juh swee*	I am
tu es *tew ay*	you are (informal singular)
il/elle est *eel/el ay*	he/she is
nous sommes *noo som*	we are
vous êtes *voo zet*	you are (formal singular or plural)
ils/elles sont *eel/el soñ*	they are

Je suis anglaise.
juh swee zonglayz
I'm English.

Je suis fatigué(e). *juh swee fatigay*	I'm tired.

Elle est heureuse? *el ay tururz*	Is she happy?

Nous sommes français. *noo som froñsay*	We're French.

3 Avoir: to have (5 minutes)

Practise **avoir** (*to have*) and the sample sentences, then test yourself.

I have	**j'ai** *jay*
you have (informal singular)	**tu as** *tew ah*
he/she has	**il/elle a** *eel/el ah*
we have	**nous avons** *noo zavoñ*
you have (formal singular or plural)	**vous avez** *voo zavay*
they have	**ils/elles ont** *eel/el zoñ*

Il a deux baguettes.
eel ah duh baget
He has two baguettes.

He has a meeting.	**Il a un rendez-vous.** *eel ah uñ roñday-voo*
Do you have a mobile phone?	**Vous avez un portable?** *voo zavay uñ portabluh*
How many brothers and sisters do you have?	**Vous avez combien de frères et sœurs?** *voo zavay koñbyañ duh frair ay sur*

4 Negatives (4 minutes)

To make a sentence negative in French, put **ne** in front of the verb and **pas** just after: **nous ne sommes pas anglais** (*we are not English*). If **ne** is followed by a vowel, it becomes **n'**: **je n'ai pas d'enfants** (*I don't have any children*). But many French people drop the **ne** when they're talking, so you'll just hear **nous sommes pas** (*we aren't*), **j'ai pas** (*I haven't*), and so on. Read these sentences aloud, then cover the French with the flap and test yourself.

le vélo
luh vayloe
bicycle

He's not married.	**Il n'est pas marié.** *eel nay pah mariyay*
I am not sure.	**Je ne suis pas sûr(e).** *juh nuh swee pah syur*
We don't have any children.	**Nous n'avons pas d'enfants.** *noo navoñ pah doñfoñ*

Je n'ai pas de voiture.
juh nay pas duh vwatyur
I don't have a car.

RÉVISEZ ET RÉPÉTEZ
Review and repeat

① How many?

❶ **trois**
trwah

❷ **neuf**
nurf

❸ **quatre**
katruh

❹ **deux**
duh

❺ **huit**
weet

❻ **dix**
dees

❼ **cinq**
sank

❽ **sept**
set

❾ **six**
sees

① How many? (2 minutes)

Cover the answers with the flap. Then say these French numbers out loud. Check you have remembered the French correctly.

3 ❷ 9 ❸ 4
❶
2 ❹ ❺ 8 10 ❻
5 ❼ 7 6
❽ ❾

② Hello

❶ **Bonjour. Je m'appelle... [your name].**
boñjoor. juh mapell...

❷ **Enchanté(e).**
oñshontay

❸ **Oui, et j'ai deux fils. Et vous?**
wee, ay jay duh fees. ay voo

❹ **Au revoir. A demain.**
ovwar. ah dumañ

② Hello (4 minutes)

You meet someone in a formal situation. Join in the conversation, replying in French according to the English prompts.

Bonjour. Je m'appelle Nicole.
❶ Answer the greeting and give your name.
Voici mon mari, Henri.
❷ Say "Pleased to meet you".
Vous êtes marié(e)?
❸ Say "Yes, and I have two sons. And you?"
Nous avons trois filles.
❹ Say "Goodbye. See you tomorrow".

3 To have or be (5 minutes)

Fill in the blanks with the correct form of **avoir** (*to have*) or **être** (*to be*). Check you have remembered the French correctly.

❶ Je _____ anglaise.

❷ Nous _____ quatre enfants.

❸ Elle _____ une belle-fille.

❹ Vous _____ rendez-vous?

❺ Il n' _____ pas fatigué.

❻ Je n' _____ pas de portable.

❼ Tu n' _____ pas sûr?

❽ Nous _____ français.

3 To have or be

❶ **suis**
swee

❷ **avons**
avoñ

❸ **a**
ah

❹ **avez**
avay

❺ **est**
ay

❻ **ai**
ay

❼ **es**
ay

❽ **sommes**
som

4 Family (4 minutes)

Say the French for each of the numbered family members. Check you have remembered the French correctly.

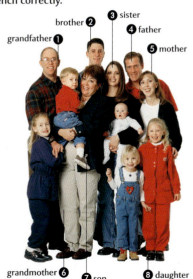

grandfather ❶
brother ❷
❸ sister
❹ father
❺ mother
grandmother ❻
❼ son
❽ daughter

4 Family

❶ **le grand-père**
luh groñpair

❷ **le frère**
luh frair

❸ **la soeur**
lah sur

❹ **le père**
luh pair

❺ **la mère**
lah mair

❻ **la grand-mère**
lah groñmair

❼ **le fils**
luh fees

❽ **la fille**
lah feeyuh

① **Warm up** (1 minute)

Count to ten (pp.10–11).

Remind yourself how to say "hello" and "goodbye". (pp.8–9)

Ask "Do you have a baguette?" (pp.14–15)

AU CAFÉ
In the café

In a typical French café you can either sit at the counter, which is cheaper, or have waiter service at a table. Tipping is the norm if you're happy with the service, but a few coins will be enough. Food is not usually served, although you can often get bread and croissants in the mornings.

② **Words to remember** (5 minutes)

Look at the words below and say them out loud a few times. Cover the French with the flap and try to remember the French for each item. Practise the words on the picture also.

la confiture
lah coñfeetyur
jam

le café crème *luh kafay krem*	coffee with frothy milk
le grand café *luh groñ kafay*	large black coffee
le thé *luh tay*	black tea
le thé au lait *luh tay oh lay*	tea with milk

le café
luh cafeh
small black coffee

le sucre
luh sookruh
sugar

Cultural tip A standard coffee is small and black. You'll need to ask if you want it any other way. If you like milk in your tea, you'll need to specify cold milk (**lait froid/** lay frwah), otherwise you are likely to get a jug of hot milk.

③ **In conversation** (4 minutes)

Bonjour. Je voudrais un café au lait, s'il vous plaît.
bonjoor. juh voodray uñ kafay oh lay, seel voo play

Hello. I would like a white coffee, please.

C'est tout madame?
say too ma-dam

Is that all madam?

Vous avez des croissants?
voo zavay day krossoñ

Do you have any croissants?

4 Useful phrases (5 minutes)

Learn these phrases. Read the English under the pictures and say the phrase in French as shown on the right. Then conceal the French with the cover flap and test yourself.

le pain
luh pañ
bread

I'd like a large black coffee, please.

Je voudrais un grand café, s'il vous plaît.
juh voodray uñ groñ kafay, seel voo play

Is that all?

C'est tout?
say too

I'll have a croissant.

Je prends un croissant.
juh pron uñ krossoñ

le café au lait
luh kafay oh lay
large coffee with milk

How much is that?

C'est combien?
say koñbyañ

Oui, bien sûr.
wee, byañ syur

Yes, certainly.

Alors deux croissants. C'est combien?
alor duh krossoñ. say koñbyañ

Two croissants then. How much is that?

Quatre euros, s'il vous plaît.
katruh uroh, seel voo play

Four euros, please.

AU RESTAURANT
In the restaurant

1 **Warm up** (1 minute)

Say "I'd like".
(pp.18-19)

Say "I don't have a
brother". (pp.14-15)

Ask "Do you have any
croissants?" (pp.18-19)

There is a variety of different types of eating place in France. In a **café** you can find a few snacks. A **brasserie** is a traditional restaurant; the service is fast and there's usually no need to book. In the more formal gastronomic restaurants, it is necessary to book and to dress smartly.

2 **Words to remember** (3 minutes)

Memorize these words. Conceal the French with the cover flap and test yourself.

la carte *lah kart*	menu
la carte des vins *lah kart day vañ*	wine list
les entrées (f) *lay zontray*	starters
les plats (m) *lay plah*	main courses
les desserts (m) *lay dessair*	desserts
le déjeuner *luh dayjunay*	lunch
le dîner *luh deenay*	dinner
le petit-déjeuner *luh puhtee dayjunay*	breakfast

cup 7

saucer 8

5 spoon

6 knife

fork 4

3 **In conversation** (4 minutes)

Bonjour. Je voudrais une table pour quatre.
boñjoor. juh voodray oon tabluh poor katruh

Hello. I would like a table for four.

Vous avez une réservation?
voo zavay oon raysairvasyoñ

Do you have a reservation?

Oui, au nom de Smith.
wee, oh noñ duh Smith

Yes, in the name of Smith.

4 Match and repeat (5 minutes)

Look at the numbered items in this table setting and match them with the French words on the right. Read the French words aloud. Now, conceal the French with the cover flap and test yourself.

glass ❶

❷ napkin

plate ❸

❶ **le verre**
luh vair

❷ **la serviette**
lah sairvyet

❸ **l'assiette** (f)
lasyet

❹ **la fourchette**
lah forshet

❺ **la cuillère**
lah kweeyair

❻ **le couteau**
luh kootoe

❼ **la tasse**
lah tass

❽ **la soucoupe**
lah sookoop

5 Useful phrases (2 minutes)

Learn these phrases and then test yourself using the cover flap to conceal the French.

What do you have for dessert?	**Qu'est ce que vous avez comme dessert?** *keskuh voo zavay kom dessair*
The bill, please.	**L'addition, s'il vous plaît.** *ladeesyoñ, seel voo play*

D'accord. Quelle table vous préférez?
dakor. kel tabluh voo prayfayray

Fine. Which table would you like?

Près de la fenêtre, s'il vous plaît.
pray duh lah fenetruh, seel voo play

Near the window, please.

Mais bien sûr. Suivez-moi.
may byañ syur. sweevay mwah

But of course. Follow me.

What are "breakfast", "lunch", and "dinner" in French? (pp.20-1)

Say "I", "you" (informal), "he", "she", "we", "you" (plural/formal), "they" (masculine), "they" (feminine). (pp.14-15)

VOULOIR
To want

In this section, you will learn the present tense of a verb that is essential to everyday conversation - **vouloir** (*to want*) - as well as a useful polite form, **je voudrais** (*I would like*). Remember to use this form when requesting something because **je veux** (*I want*) may sound too strong.

2 **Vouloir: to want** (6 minutes)

Say the different forms of **vouloir** (*to want*) aloud. Use the cover flaps to test yourself and, when you are confident, practise the sample sentences below.

je veux *juh vuh*	I want
tu veux *tew vuh*	you want (informal)
il/elle veut *eel/el vuh*	he/she wants
nous voulons *noo vooloñ*	we want
vous voulez *voo voolay*	you want (formal/plural)
ils/elles veulent *eel/el verl*	they want
Tu veux du vin? *tew vuh dew vañ*	Do you want some wine?
Elle veut une nouvelle voiture. *el vuh oon noovel vwatyur*	She wants a new car.
Nous voulons aller en vacances. *noo vooloñ zallay oñ vakons*	We want to go on holiday.

Je veux des bonbons.
juh vuh day boñ-boñ
I want some sweets.

Conversational tip To say *some*, **de** (*of*) combines with **le**, **la**, or **les** to produce **du** for the masculine, **de la** for feminine, or **des** for the plural, as in **du café**, **de la confiture**, and **des citrons** (*lemons*). If the sentence is negative, use only **de**, as in **Il n'y a pas de café**. In the same way, **à** (*to*) combines with **le**, **la**, or **les** to produce **au** for the masculine, **à la** for the feminine, and **aux** for the plural.

3 Polite requests (4 minutes)

There is a form of **je veux** (*I want*) used for polite requests: **je voudrais**. Practise the sentences below and then test yourself.

I'd like a beer, please.
Je voudrais une bière, s'il vous plaît.
juh voodray oon biyair, seel voo play

I'd like a table for tonight.
Je voudrais une table pour ce soir.
juh voodray oon tabluh poor suh swar

I'd like the menu.
Je voudrais la carte.
juh voodray lah kart

4 Put into practice (4 minutes)

Join in this conversation. Read the French beside the pictures on the left and then follow the English prompts to make your reply in French. Test yourself by concealing the answers with the cover flap.

Bonsoir, madame. Vous avez une réservation?
boñswar, ma-dam. Voo zavay oon raysairvasyoñ

Good evening, madam. Do you have a reservation?

Say: No, but I would like a table for three, please.

Non, mais je voudrais une table pour trois, s'il vous plaît.
noñ, may juh voodray oon tabluh poor trwah, seel voo play

Quelle table vous préférez?
kel tabluh voo prayfayray

Which table would you like?

Say: Near the window, please.

Près de la fenêtre, s'il vous plaît.
pray duh lah fenetruh, seel voo play

1 **Warm up** (1 minute)

Say "I'm tired" and "I'm not sure". (pp.14–15)

Ask "Do you have croissants?" (pp.18–19)

Say "I'd like a white coffee". (pp.18–19)

LES PLATS
Dishes

France is famous for its cuisine and the quality of its best restaurants. It also offers a wide variety of regional dishes. Plenty of garlic and butter are a feature of many typical dishes. Although traditionally French cuisine is meat-based, many restaurants now offer a vegetarian menu.

Cultural tip You will usually have the choice of eating a set **menu** or ordering **à la carte**. With a set menu, salad is often a starter and you usually have to choose between dessert or cheese.

2 **Match and repeat** (4 minutes)

Look at the numbered items and match them to the French words in the panel on the left. Test yourself using the cover flap.

❶ **les légumes** (m)
lay laygoom

❷ **le fruit**
luh froo-wee

❸ **le fromage**
luh fromarj

❹ **les noix** (f)
lay nwah

❺ **la soupe**
lah soop

❻ **la volaille**
lah vol-eye

❼ **le poisson**
luh pwassoñ

❽ **les pâtes** (f)
lay pat

❾ **les fruits de mer** (m)
lay froo-wee duh mair

❿ **la viande**
lah vee-ond

fruit ❷

vegetables ❶

cheese ❸

❺ soup

poultry ❻

❽ pasta

❾ seafood

3 Words to remember: cooking methods (3 minutes)

Familiarize yourself with these words and then test yourself.

fried	**frit(e)**	*free(t)*
grilled	**grillé(e)**	*greeyay*
roasted	**rôti(e)**	*rotee*
boiled	**bouilli(e)**	*booyee*
steamed	**à la vapeur**	*ah lah vapur*
rare	**saignant(e)**	*say-nyoñ(t)*

Je voudrais mon steak bien cuit.
juh voodray moñ stayk byañ kwee
I'd like my steak well done.

6 Say it (2 minutes)

What is **cassoulet**?

I'm allergic to seafood.

I'd like a beer.

4 Words to remember: drinks (3 minutes)

Familiarize yourself with these words.

water	**l'eau** (f)	*loe*
fizzy water	**l'eau gazeuse** (f)	*loe gazuz*
still water	**l'eau plate** (f)	*loe plat*
wine	**le vin**	*luh vañ*
beer	**la bière**	*lah biyair*
fruit juice	**le jus de fruits**	*luh joo duh froo-wee*

nuts

fish

5 Useful phrases (2 minutes)

Learn these phrases and then test yourself.

I'm a vegetarian	**Je suis végétarien.**	*juh swee vejitah-ryañ*
I'm allergic to nuts.	**Je suis allergique aux noix.**	*juh swee zalurzheek oh nwah*
What are "escargots"?	**Qu'est que c'est les "escargots"?**	*keskuh say lay zeskargoh*

 meat

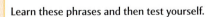

RÉVISEZ ET RÉPÉTEZ
Review and repeat

1 At table

❶ **les noix**
lay nwah

❷ **les fruits de mer**
lay froo-wee duh mair

❸ **la viande**
lah vee-ond

❹ **le sucre**
luh sookruh

❺ **le verre**
luh vair

1 At table (4 minutes)

Name the numbered items.

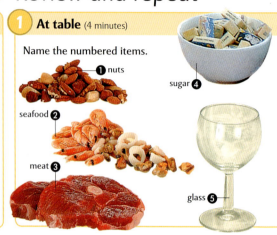

❶ nuts
sugar ❹
seafood ❷
meat ❸
glass ❺

2 This is my...

❶ **C'est mon mari.**
say moñ maree

❷ **Voici ma fille.**
vwasee mah feeyuh

❸ **Ma table est non-fumeur.**
mah tabluh ay noñ-foomur

❹ **Mes enfants sont fatigués.**
may zoñfoñ soñ fatigay

2 This is my... (4 minutes)

Say these phrases in French.
Use **mon**, **ma**, or **mes**.

❶ This is my husband.

❷ Here is my daughter.

❸ My table is non-smoking.

❹ My children are tired.

3 I'd like...

❶ **Je voudrais un café.**
juh voodray uñ kafay

❷ **Je voudrais de la confiture.**
juh voodray duh lah coñfeetyur

❸ **Je voudrais du pain.**
juh voodray doo pañ

❹ **Je voudrais un café au lait.**
juh voodray uñ kafay oh lay

3 I'd like... (3 minutes)

Say you'd like the following:

bread ❸
jam ❷
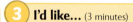

❶ black coffee
large coffee ❹ with milk

⑥ pasta

knife ⑦

⑧ cheese

beer ⑩

⑨ napkin

Réponses
Answers (Cover with flap)

① At table

⑥ **les pâtes**
lay pat

⑦ **le couteau**
luh kootoe

⑧ **le fromage**
luh fromarj

⑨ **la serviette**
lah sairvyet

⑩ **la bière**
lah biyair

④ Restaurant (4 minutes)

You arrive at a restaurant. Join in the conversation, replying in French according to the English prompts.

Bonjour madame, monsieur.
① Ask for a table for six.

Fumeur ou non-fumeur?
② Say: non-smoking.

Suivez-moi, s'il vous plaît.
③ Ask for the menu.

Et vous voulez la carte des vins?
④ Say: No. Fizzy water, please.

Voilà.
⑤ Say: I don't have a glass.

④ Restaurant

① **Bonjour. Je voudrais une table pour six.**
boñjoor. juh voodray oon tabluh por sees

② **Non-fumeur.**
noñ-foomur

③ **La carte, s'il vous plaît.**
lah kart, seel voo play

④ **Non. De l'eau gazeuse, s'il vous plaît.**
noñ. duh loe gazuz, seel voo play

⑤ **Je n'ai pas de verre.**
juh nay pah duh vair

1 Warm up (1 minute)

Say "he is" and "they are". (pp.14-15)

Say "he is not" and "they are not". (pp.14-15)

What is French for "the children"? (pp.10-11)

LES JOURS ET LES MOIS
Days and months

In French the *days of the week* (**les jours de semaine**) and *months* (**les mois**) do not have capital letters. The months have similar names to the English. You use **en** with months: **en avril** (*in April*), but not with days.

2 Words to remember: days (5 minutes)

Familiarize yourself with these words and test yourself using the flap.

lundi *luñdee*	Monday
mardi *mardee*	Tuesday
mercredi *mairkrudee*	Wednesday
jeudi *jurdee*	Thursday
vendredi *voñdrudee*	Friday
samedi *samdee*	Saturday
dimanche *deemonsh*	Sunday
aujourd'hui *oh-joordwee*	today
demain *dumañ*	tomorrow
hier *eeyair*	yesterday

Demain, c'est lundi.
dumañ, say luñdee
Tomorrow is Monday.

3 Useful phrases: days (2 minutes)

Learn these phrases and then test yourself using the cover flap.

La réunion n'est pas mardi. *lah rayoonyoñ nay pah mardee*	The meeting isn't on Tuesday.
Je travaille le dimanche. *juh trav-eye luh deemonsh*	I work on Sundays.

4 Words to remember: months (5 minutes)

Familiarize yourself with these words and test yourself using the flap.

Notre anniversaire de mariage est en juillet.
notruh aneevairsair duh mareeaj ay toñ jweeyay
Our wedding anniversary is in July.

Noël est en décembre.
nowel ay toñ daysombruh
Christmas is in December.

January	**janvier**	*joñvyay*
February	**février**	*fevreeyay*
March	**mars**	*mars*
April	**avril**	*avreel*
May	**mai**	*may*
June	**juin**	*jwañ*
July	**juillet**	*jweeyay*
August	**août**	*oot*
September	**septembre**	*septombruh*
October	**octobre**	*oktobruh*
November	**novembre**	*novombruh*
December	**décembre**	*daysombruh*
month	**le mois**	*luh mwah*
year	**l'an** (m)	*loñ*

5 Useful phrases: months (2 minutes)

Learn these phrases and then test yourself using the cover flap.

My children are on holiday in August.
Mes enfants sont en vacances en août.
may zoñfoñ soñ toñ vakons oñ oot

My birthday is in June.
Mon anniversaire est en juin.
moñ naneevairsair ay toñ jwañ

L'HEURE ET LES NOMBRES
Time and numbers

1 **Warm up** (1 minute)

Count in French from
1 to 10. (pp.10-11)

Say "I have a reservation".
(pp.20-1)

Say "The meeting is on
Wednesday". (pp.28-9)

The 12-hour clock is used in everyday speech while
the 24-hour clock is employed in stations and airports,
etc. While in English the minutes are first (*ten to five*),
in French the hour is first: **dix heures moins cinq**
(*ten minus five*).

2 **Words to remember: time** (4 minutes)

Memorize how to tell the time in French.

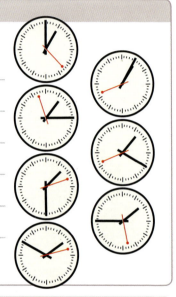

une heure *oon ur*	one o'clock
une heure cinq *oon ur sank*	five past one
une heure et quart *oon ur ay kar*	quarter past one
une heure vingt *oon ur vañ*	twenty past one
une heure et demie *oon ur ay dumee*	half past one
deux heures moins le quart *duh zur mwañ luh kar*	quarter to two
deux heures moins dix *duh zur mwañ dees*	ten to two

3 **Useful phrases** (2 minutes)

Learn these phrases and then test yourself using
the cover flap.

Quelle heure est-il? *kel ur ay teel*	What time is it?

A quelle heure voulez-vous le petit déjeuner? *ah kel ur voolay voo luh puhtee dayjunay*	What time do you want breakfast?

J'ai une réservation pour douze heures. *jay oon raysairvasyoñ poor dooz ur*	I have a reservation for twelve o'clock.

4 Words to remember: higher numbers (6 minutes)

In French when you say 21, 31, etc. you say: **vingt-et-un**, **trente-et-un**, and so on. After that just put the numbers together without **et**: **vingt-deux** (22), **quarante-cinq** (45).

70 is **soixante-dix** (*sixty-ten*), 75 is **soixante-quinze** (*sixty-fifteen*), and so on. **Quatre-vingt** (80) means *four-twenties*, and 90 is **quatre-vingt-dix** (*four-twenties-ten*). So 82 is **quatre-vingt-deux** and 97 is **quatre-vingt-dix-sept**.

Ça fait quatre-vingt-cinq euros.
sah fay katruh-vañ-sank uroh
That's eighty-five euros.

eleven	**onze**	*onz*
twelve	**douze**	*dooz*
thirteen	**treize**	*trez*
fourteen	**quatorze**	*katorz*
fifteen	**quinze**	*kanz*
sixteen	**seize**	*sez*
seventeen	**dix-sept**	*deeset*
eighteen	**dix-huit**	*deezweet*
nineteen	**dix-neuf**	*deeznurf*
twenty	**vingt**	*vañ*
thirty	**trente**	*tront*
forty	**quarante**	*karont*
fifty	**cinquante**	*sankont*
sixty	**soixante**	*swasont*
seventy	**soixante-dix**	*swasont-dees*
eighty	**quatre-vingt**	*katruh-vañ*
ninety	**quatre-vingt-dix**	*katruh-vañ-dees*
hundred	**cent**	*soñ*
three hundred	**trois cents**	*trwah soñ*
thousand	**mil**	*meel*
ten thousand	**dix mille**	*dee meel*
two hundred thousand	**deux cent mille**	*duh soñ meel*
one million	**un million**	*oon meel-yoñ*

5 Say it (2 minutes)

twenty-five

sixty-eight

eighty-four

ninety-one

five to ten.

half past eleven.

What time is lunch?

LES RENDEZ-VOUS
Appointments

Business in France is generally conducted more
formally than in Britain or the United States; always
address business contacts as **vous**. The French tend
to leave the office for the lunch hour, often having a sit-
down meal in a restaurant or, less commonly, at home.

Bienvenue.
byañvenoo
Welcome.

2 **Useful phrases** (5 minutes)

Learn these phrases and then test yourself.

Prenons rendez-vous pour demain. *prunoñ ronday-voo poor dumañ*	Let's meet tomorrow.
Avec qui? *avek kee*	With whom?
Quand êtes-vous libre? *koñ et-voo leebruh*	When are you free?
Je suis désolé(e), je suis occupé(e). *juh swee dayzolay, juh swee zokupay*	I'm sorry, I'm busy.
Pourquoi pas jeudi? *poorkwah pah jurdee*	How about Thursday?
C'est bon pour moi. *say boh poor mwah*	That's good for me.

la poignée
de main
*lah pwanyay
duh mañ*
handshake

3 **In conversation** (4 minutes)

Bonjour. J'ai rendez-vous.
boñjoor. jay ronday-voo

Hello. I have an
appointment.

Avec qui?
avek kee

With whom?

Avec Monsieur Le Blanc.
avek musyuh luh bloñ

With Mr Le Blanc.

4 Put into practice (5 minutes)

Join in this conversation. Read the French beside the pictures on the left and then follow the instructions to make your reply. Then test yourself by concealing the answers on the right with the cover flap.

Prenons rendez-vous pour jeudi.
prunoñ ronday-voo poor jurdee

Let's meet on Thursday.

Say: Sorry, I'm busy.

Je suis désolé, je suis occupé.
juh swee dayzolay, juh swee zokupay

Quand êtes-vous libre?
koñ et-voo leebruh

When are you free?

Say: Tuesday afternoon.

Mardi après-midi.
mardee apray meedee

C'est bon pour moi.
say boñ poor mwa

That's good for me.

Ask: What time?

A quelle heure?
ah kel ur

A quatre heures, si c'est bon pour vous.
ah katruh ur see say boñ poor voo

At four o'clock, if that's good for you.

Say: It's good for me.

C'est bon pour moi.
say boñ poor mwah

Très bien. A quelle heure?
tray byañ. ah kel ur

Very good. What time?

A trois heures, mais je suis un peu en retard.
ah trwah zur, may juh swee uñ puh oñ retar

At three o'clock, but I'm a little late.

Ne vous inquiétez pas. Asseyez-vous, je vous en prie.
nuh voo zañkyetay pah. assayay voo, juh voo zoñ pree

Don't worry. Sit down, please.

AU TÉLÉPHONE
On the telephone

The emergency number for police, ambulance, or fire services is 112. To make direct international calls, dial 00 followed by the country code, area code (omit the initial 0) and the number. The country code for France is 33.

2 Match and repeat (4 minutes)

Match the numbered items to the French in the panel on the left and test yourself.

❶ le chargeur
luh sharjur

❷ le téléphone
luh telayfon

❸ le répondeur
luh raypoñdur

❹ les écouteurs (m)
lay zaykootur

❺ le portable
luh portabluh

❻ la carte SIM
lah kart seem

telephone ❷

charger ❶

headphones ❹

❺ mobile

3 In conversation (4 minutes)

Allô. Pauline Du Bois à l'appareil.
aloh. pawleen doo bwah ah lap-paray

Hello. Pauline du Bois speaking.

Bonjour. Je voudrais parler à Rachid Djamal.
boñjoor. juh voodray parlay ah rasheed jahmal

Hello. I'd like to speak to Rachid Djamal.

C'est de la part de qui?
say duh lah par duh kee

Who's speaking?

SIM card 6

Je voudrais acheter une carte SIM.
juh voodray ashetay oon kart seem
I'd like to buy a SIM card.

3 answering machine

4 Useful phrases (4 minutes)

Practise these phrases. Then test yourself using the cover flap.

I'd like the number for Michel.

Je voudrais le numéro de Michel.
juh voodray luh noomairoe duh meeshell

I'd like to speak to Françoise Martin.

Je voudrais parler à Françoise Martin.
juh voodray parlay ah franswahz martañ

Can I leave a message?

Je peux laisser un message?
juh puh laysay uñ mesarj

Sorry I have the wrong number.

Désolé(e), je me suis trompé(e) de numéro.
dayzolay, juh muh swee trompay duh noomairoe

5 Say it (2 minutes)

I'd like to speak to Mr Hachart.

Can I leave a message for Emma?

Jean Leblanc de l'imprimerie Laporte.
joñ luhbloñ duh lahpreemuree laport

Jean Leblanc of Laporte Printers.

Désolée. La ligne est occupée.
dayzolay. lah leenyuh et okupay

I'm sorry. The line is busy.

Il peut me rappeller, s'il vous plaît?
eel puh muh raplay, seel voo play

Can he call me back, please?

RÉVISEZ ET RÉPÉTEZ
Review and repeat

Réponses
Answers (Cover with flap)

1 Sums

❶ **seize**
sez

❷ **trente-neuf**
tront-nurf

❸ **cinquante-trois**
sankont-trwah

❹ **soixante-quatorze**
swasont-katorz

❺ **quatre-vingt dix-neuf**
katruh-vañ deeznuf

❻ **quarante-et-un**
karont-ay-uñ

1 Sums (4 minutes)

Say the answers to these sums out loud in French. Then check you have remembered correctly.

❶ $10 + 6 = ?$
❷ $14 + 25 = ?$
❸ $66 - 13 = ?$
❹ $40 + 34 = ?$
❺ $90 + 9 = ?$
❻ $46 - 5 = ?$

3 Telephones (3 minutes)

What are the numbered items in French?

mobile ❶

headphones ❺

2 I want...

❶ **voulez**
voolay

❷ **veut**
vuh

❸ **voulons**
vooloñ

❹ **veux**
vuh

❺ **veux**
vuh

❻ **veut**
vuh

2 I want... (3 minutes)

Fill the blanks with the correct form of **vouloir**.

❶ Vous _____ un café?
❷ Elle _____ aller en vacances.
❸ Nous _____ une table pour trois.
❹ Tu _____ une bière?
❺ Je _____ une nouvelle voiture.
❻ Il _____ des bonbons.

answering **❷**
machine

SIM card **❸**

telephone **❹**

Réponses
Answers (Cover with flap)

3 Telephones

❶ le portable
luh portabluh

❷ le répondeur
luh raypoñdur

❸ la carte SIM
lah kart seem

❹ le téléphone
luh telayfon

❺ les écouteurs
lay zaykootur

---

4 When? (2 minutes)

What do these sentences mean?

❶ J'ai rendez-vous lundi vingt mai.

❷ Mon anniversaire est en septembre.

❸ Je reviens dimanche.

❹ Ils ne travaillent pas en août.

4 When?

❶ I have a meeting on Monday 20th May.

❷ My birthday is in September.

❸ I come back on Sunday.

❹ They don't work in August.

---

5 Time (3 minutes)

Say these times in French.

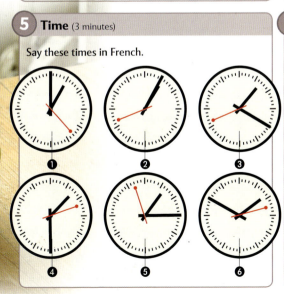

5 Time

❶ une heure
oon ur

❷ une heure cinq
oon ur sank

❸ une heure vingt
oon ur vañ

❹ une heure et demie
oon ur ay dumee

❺ une heure et quart
oon ur ay kar

❻ deux heures moins dix
duh zur mwañ dees

1 **Warm up** (1 minute)

Count to 100 in tens.
(pp.10-11, pp.30-1)

Ask "At what time?"
(pp.30-1)

Say "Half-past one".
(pp.30-1)

AU GUICHET
At the ticket office

In France, before getting on the train, you must *validate* (**composter**) your ticket by stamping it. Special orange machines are installed in every train station for this purpose. Fines are handed out to those who forget to validate their tickets. Most trains have both first and second class seats.

2 **Words to remember** (3 minutes)

Learn these words and then test yourself.

la gare *lah gar*	station
le train *luh trañ*	train
la voiture *lah vwatyur*	carriage
le billet *luh beeyay*	ticket
aller-simple *allay-sañpluh*	single
aller-retour *allay-rutoor*	return
première classe *prumyair klas*	first class
en seconde *oñ sugond*	second class

le passager
luh pasahjay
passenger

le quai
luh kay
platform

La gare est pleine de monde.
lah gar ay plen duh moñd
The station is crowded.

3 **In conversation** (4 minutes)

Deux billets pour Bordeaux s'il vous plait.
duh beeyay poor bordoe seel voo play

Two tickets for Bordeaux, please.

Aller-retour?
allay rutoor

Return?

Oui. Je dois réserver des places?
wee. juh dwah rayzurvay day plas

Yes. Do I need to reserve seats?

4 **Useful phrases** (5 minutes)

Learn these phrases and then test yourself using the cover flap.

How much is a ticket to Lille?	**C'est combien un billet pour Lille?** *say koñbyañ uñ beeyay poor leel*
Do you accept credit cards?	**Vous acceptez les cartes de crédit?** *voo zakseptay lay kart duh kredee*
Do I have to change?	**Je dois changer?** *juh dwah shonjay*
Which platform does the train leave from?	**Le train part de quel quai?** *luh trañ par duh kel kay*
Are there discounts?	**Vous faites des réductions?** *voo fet day raydooksyoñ*
What time does the train for Paris leave?	**A quelle heure part le train pour Paris?** *ah kel ur par luh trañ poor paree*

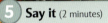

Le train pour Poitiers est annulé.
luh trañ poor pwatyer et anulay
The train for Poitiers is cancelled.

5 **Say it** (2 minutes)

Which platform does the train for Paris leave from?

Three tickets to Lyon, please.

Cultural tip Most train stations have automatic ticket machines that accept credit and debit cards as well as cash.

Ce n'est pas nécessaire. Quarante euros s'il vous plaît.
suh nay pah nesaysair. karont uroh seel voo play

That's not necessary. Forty euros please.

Vous acceptez les cartes de crédit?
voo zakseptay lay kart duh kredee

Do you accept credit cards?

Bien sûr. Le train part du quai numéro cinq.
byañ syur. luh trañ par doo kay noomairoe sank

Certainly. The train leaves from platform five.

1 **Warm up** (1 minute)

How do you say "train"?
(pp.38-9)

What does "Le train part
de quel quai?" mean?
(pp.38-9)

Ask "When are you
free?" (pp.32-3)

ALLER ET PRENDRE
To go and to take

Aller (to go) and **prendre** (to take) are essential verbs in French. You can also use **prendre** to say I'll have (**je prends**) when you talk about food and drink. Note that the present tense in French includes the sense of a continuous action – for example, **je vais** means both I go and I am going.

2 **Aller: to go** (6 minutes)

Say the different forms of **aller** (to go) aloud. Use the flaps to test yourself and, when you are confident, practise the sample sentences below.

je vais *juh vay*	I go
tu vas *tew vah*	you go (informal singular)
il/elle va *eel/el vah*	he/she goes
nous allons *noo zalloñ*	we go
vous allez *voo zallay*	you go (formal singular or plural)
ils/elles vont *eel/el voñ*	they go

Où allez-vous? *oo allay voo*	Where are you going?
Je vais à Paris. *juh vay zah paree*	I'm going to Paris.
Nous allons à l'école en train. *noo zalloñ ah laykoloñ trañ*	We go to school by train.

Je vais à la Tour Eiffel.
juh vay zah lah toor eefel
I'm going to the Eiffel Tower.

Cultural tip The **TGV (train à grande vitesse)** is a fast train that can get you from Paris to the south of France in about three hours. Generally you will need to reserve a seat and can still choose smoking or non-smoking seats. **TER (trains express régionaux)** is another type of fast train. These trains are cheaper than the **TGV**. You can buy a ticket on the day of travel and get on without a reservation.

3 Prendre: to take (6 minutes)

Je prends le métro tous les jours.
juh proñ luh metroe too lay joor
I take the metro every day.

Say the different forms of **prendre** (*to take*) aloud. Use the flaps to cover the French and test yourself. When you are confident, practise the sample sentences below.

je prends *juh proñ*	I take
tu prends *tew proñ*	you take (informal singular)
il/elle prend *eel/el proñ*	he/she takes
nous prenons *noo prunoñ*	we take
vous prenez *voo prunay*	you take (formal singular or plural)
ils/elles prennent *eel/el pren*	they take

Je ne veux pas prendre un taxi. *juh nuh vuh pah proñdruh uñ taksee*	I don't want to take a taxi.
Prenez la première à gauche. *prunay lah prumyair ah gaush*	Take the first on the left.
Il prend le bœuf bourguignon. *eel proñ luh buf boorgheenyoñ*	He'll have the beef bourguignon.

4 Put into practice (2 minutes)

Cover the text on the right and complete the dialogue in French.

Où allez-vous? *oo allay voo*	**Je vais au Louvre.** *juh vay zoh loovruh*

Where are you going?

Say: I'm going to the Louvre.

Vous voulez prendre le métro? *voo voolay proñdruh luh metroe*	**Non, je veux aller en bus.** *noñ. juh vuh allay oñ boos*

Do you want to take the metro?

Say: No, I want to go by bus.

Warm up (1 minute)

Say "I'd like to go to the station". (pp.40-1)

Ask "Where are you going?" (pp.40-1)

Say "fruit" and "cheese". (pp.24-5).

TAXI, BUS, ET MÉTRO
Taxi, bus, and metro

With buses, as with trains, you need to validate your ticket in a machine at the time of travel. For the metro, there's a standard fare and you can also buy a **carnet**, a book of 10 tickets. It's unusual to flag down a taxi in the street. You need to find one of the many taxi ranks and wait there.

2 **Words to remember** (4 minutes)

Familiarize yourself with these words.

le bus *luh boos*	bus
le car *luh kar*	coach
la gare routière *lah gar rootyair*	bus station
l'arrêt de bus (m) *laray duh boos*	bus stop
le tarif *luh tareef*	fare
le taxi *luh taksee*	taxi
la rangée de taxis *lah roñjay duh taksee*	taxi rank
la station de métro *lah stasyoñ duh metroe*	metro station

Le bus numéro 4 s'arrête ici?
luh boos noomairoe katruh saret eesee
Does the number 4 bus stop here?

3 **In conversation: taxi** (2 minutes)

Le marché aux fromages, s'il vous plaît.
luh marshayoe fromarj, seel voo play

The cheese market, please.

Oui, sans problème, monsieur.
wee. soñ problem musyuh

Yes, no problem, sir.

Vous pouvez me déposer ici, s'il vous plaît?
voo poovay muh dayposay eesee, seel voo play

Can you drop me here, please?

4 Useful phrases (4 minutes)

Learn these phrases and then test yourself using the cover flap.

I want a taxi to the Arc de Triomphe.	**Je veux un taxi pour l'Arc de Triomphe.** *juh vuh uh taksee poor lark duh treeoñf*
When is the next bus to the station?	**Quand est le prochain bus pour la gare?** *koñ ay luh proshen boos poor lah gar*
How do you get to the museum?	**Pour aller au musée?** *poor allay oh moozay*
How long is the journey?	**Le trajet dure combien de temps?** *luh trajay dyur koñbyañ duh toñ*
Please wait for me.	**Attendez-moi s'il vous plaît.** *atonday-mwah seel voo play*

Cultural tip Métro lines (**lignes**) in Paris are known by the names of the first and last stations on the line. Follow the signs to the relevant end station – for example, direction Porte d'Orléans. Look out for the beautiful art deco Métropolitain signs retained in some stations.

6 Say it (2 minutes)

Do you go near the train station?

The fruit market, please.

When's the next coach to Calais?

5 In conversation: bus (2 minutes)

Vous allez près du musée?
vooz allay pray doo moozay

Do you go near the museum?

Oui. Ça fait quatre-vingt centimes.
wee. sah fay katruh vañ sonteem

Yes. That's 80 cents.

Dites-moi quand on arrive, s'il vous plaît.
deet mwah koñ toñ areev, seel voo play

Tell me when we arrive, please.

1 **Warm up** (1 minute)

How do you say "I have..."? (pp.14-15)

Say "my father", "my sister", and "my parents". (pp.16-17)

Say "I'm going to Paris". (pp.40-1)

EN ROUTE
On the road

Be sure to familiarize yourself with the French rules of the road before driving in France. French **autoroutes** (*motorways*) are fast but expensive. They are toll (**péage**) roads in which you usually take a ticket as you join the motorway and pay according to the distance travelled as you leave it.

2 **Match and repeat** (4 minutes)

Match the numbered items to the list on the left, then test yourself.

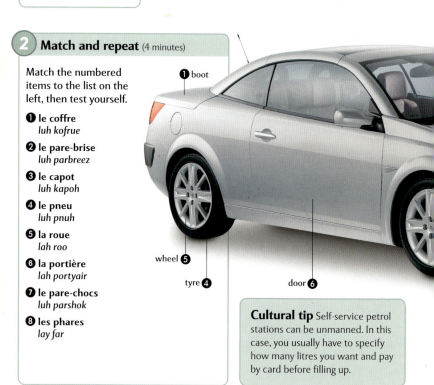

❶ **boot**

❺ **wheel**

❹ **tyre**

❻ **door**

❶ **le coffre**
luh kofrue

❷ **le pare-brise**
luh parbreez

❸ **le capot**
luh kapoh

❹ **le pneu**
luh pnuh

❺ **la roue**
lah roo

❻ **la portière**
lah portyair

❼ **le pare-chocs**
luh parshok

❽ **les phares**
lay far

Cultural tip Self-service petrol stations can be unmanned. In this case, you usually have to specify how many litres you want and pay by card before filling up.

3 **Road signs** (2 minutes)

Sens unique
sons ooneek

One way

Rond-point
roñ pwañ

Roundabout

CÉDEZ LE PASSAGE

Cédez le passage
seday luh passarj

Give way

4 **Useful phrases** (4 minutes)

Learn these phrases and then test yourself using the cover flap.

My indicator doesn't work. **Mon clignotant ne marche pas.**
moñ kleenyoe-toñ nuh marsh pah

Fill it up, please. **Le plein, s'il vous plaît.**
luh plañ, seel voo play

❷ windscreen

❸ bonnet

headlights ❽   ❼ bumper

5 **Words to remember** (3 minutes)

Familiarize yourself with these words then test yourself using the flap.

car	**la voiture** *lah vwatyur*
petrol	**l'essence** (f) *laysans*
diesel	**le gazole** *luh gazol*
oil	**l'huile** (f) *lweel*
engine	**le moteur** *luh motur*
gearbox	**la boîte de vitesses** *lah bwat duh veetess*
flat tyre	**le pneu crevé** *luh pnuh kruvay*
exhaust	**le pot d'échappement** *luh poe dayshapmoñ*
driving licence	**le permis de conduire** *luh pairmee duh kondweer*

6 **Say it** (1 minute)

My gearbox doesn't work.

I have a flat tyre.

Passage protégé
passarj protayjay

Priority road

Sens interdit
sons añtairdee

No entry

Défense de stationner
dayfoñs duh stahseeonay

No parking

Réponses
Answers Cover with flap

RÉVISEZ ET RÉPÉTEZ
Review and repeat

1 Transport

❶ **le bus**
luh boos

❷ **le taxi**
luh taksee

❸ **la voiture**
lah vwatyur

❹ **le train**
luh trañ

❺ **le vélo**
luh vayloe

❻ **le métro**
luh metroe

1 Transport (3 minutes)

Name these forms of transport in French.

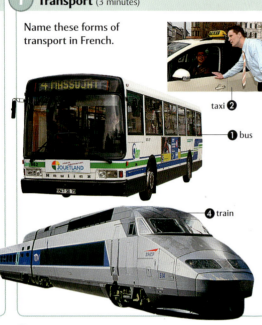

taxi ❷

❶ bus

❹ train

2 Go and take

❶ **allons**
alloñ

❷ **vais**
vay

❸ **prend**
proñ

❹ **allez**
allay

❺ **prenez**
prunay

❻ **prends**
proñ

2 Go and take (4 minutes)

Use the correct form of the verb in brackets.

❶ Nous ____ à la Tour Eiffel. (aller)

❷ Je ____ à la gare. (aller)

❸ Elle ____ rendez-vous lundi. (prendre)

❹ Où ____-vous? (aller)

❺ Que ____-vous? (prendre)

❻ Je ____ le bœuf. (prendre)

3 Vous or tu?
(4 minutes)

Use the correct form of you.

❶ You are in a café. Ask "Do you have croissants?"

❷ You are with a friend. Ask "Do you want a beer?"

❸ A business woman approaches you at your company reception. Ask "Do you have an appointment?"

❹ You are on the bus. Ask "Do you go near the station?"

❺ Ask your mother where she's going tomorrow.

❻ Ask your client "Are you free on Wednesday?"

Réponses
Answers Cover with flap

3 Vous or tu?

❶ **Vous avez des croissants?**
voo zavay day krossoñ

❷ **Tu veux une bière?**
tew vuh oon biyair

❸ **Vous avez rendez-vous?**
voo zavay roñday voo

❹ **Vous allez près de la gare?**
voo zallay pray duh lah gar

❺ **Où vas-tu demain?**
oo vah-tew dumañ

❻ **Vous êtes libre mercredi?**
voo zet leebruh mairkrudee

❸ car

❺ bicycle

❻ metro

4 Tickets (4 minutes)

You're buying tickets at a train station. Follow the conversation, replying in French following the numbered English prompts.

Je peux vous aider?
❶ I'd like two tickets to Lille.

Aller-simple ou aller-retour?
❷ Return, please.

Voilà. Cinquante euros, s'il vous plaît.
❸ What time does the train leave?

A treize heures dix.
❹ What platform does the train leave from?

Quai numéro sept.
❺ Thank you. Goodbye.

4 Tickets

❶ **Je voudrais deux billets pour Lille.**
juh voodray duh beeyay poor leel

❷ **Aller-retour, s'il vous plaît.**
allay rutoor, seel voo play

❸ **A quelle heure part le train?**
ah kel ur par luh trañ

❹ **Le train part de quel quai?**
luh trañ par duh kel kay

❺ **Merci. Au revoir.**
mairsee. ovwar

EN VILLE
About town

Most French towns still have a market day and a thriving community of small shops. Even small villages usually have a mayor and a town hall. There may be parking restrictions in the town centre. Look out for signs for **parcmètres** (*pay and display*) and **défense de stationner** (*parking forbidden*).

1 **Warm up** (1 minute)

Ask "How do you get to the musuem?" (pp.42-3)

Say "I want to take the metro" and "I don't want to take a taxi". (pp.40-1)

2 **Match and repeat** (4 minutes)

Match the numbered locations to the words in the panel.

❶ **la mairie**
lah mayree

❷ **le pont**
luh poñ

❸ **le centre ville**
luh sontruh veel

❹ **l'église** (f)
legleez

❺ **le parking**
luh parking

❻ **la place**
lah plas

❼ **la galerie d'art**
lah galree dar

❽ **le musée**
luh moozay

church ❹

town hall ❶

bridge ❷

3 **Words to remember** (4 minutes)

Familiarize yourself with these words and test yourself using the cover flap.

la station service *la stasyoñ servees*	petrol station
le syndicat d'initiative *luh sañdeekar deeneesyateev*	tourist information
le garage *luh gararj*	car repair shop
la piscine municipale *lah piseen mooneeseepal*	public swimming pool

❼ art gallery

4 Useful phrases (4 minutes)

La cathédrale est au centre-ville
lah kataydral et oh sontruh veel
The cathedral is in the town centre.

Learn these phrases and then test yourself using the cover flap.

Is there an art gallery in town?	**Il y a une galerie d'art en ville?** *eelyah oon galree dar oñ veel*
Is it far from here?	**C'est loin d'ici?** *say lwañ deesee*
There is a swimming pool near the bridge.	**Il y a une piscine près du pont.** *eelyah oon piseen pray doo poñ*
There isn't a library.	**Il n'y a pas de bibliothèque.** *eenyah pah duh bib-lee-yotek*

5 Put into practice (2 minutes)

car park ❺

❸ town centre

❻ square

museum ❽

Join in this conversation. Read the French on the left and follow the instructions to make your reply. Then test yourself by concealing the answers with the cover flap.

Je peux vous aider? *juh puh voo zeday* Can I help you? Ask: Is there a library in town?	**Il y a une bibliothèque en ville?** *eelyah oon bib-lee-yotek oñ veel*
Non, mais il ya un musée. *noñ may eelyah uñ moozay* No, but there's a museum. Ask: How do I get to the museum?	**Pour aller au musée?** *poor allay oh moozay*
C'est là-bas. *say lah bah* It's over there. Say: Thank you very much.	**Merci beaucoup.** *mairsee bohkoo*

LES DIRECTIONS
Finding your way

1 Warm up (1 minute)

How do you say "near to the station"? (pp.42-3)

Say "Take the first on the left". (pp.40-1)

Ask "Where are you going?" (pp.40-1)

To help you find your way, you'll often find a **plan de la ville** (*town plan*) situated in the town, usually near the town hall or tourist office. In the older parts of French towns there are often narrow streets, in which you will usually find a one-way system in operation. Parking is usually restricted.

2 Useful phrases (4 minutes)

Learn these phrases and then test yourself.

tournez à gauche/droite *toornay ah gaush/dwrat*	turn left/right
sur la gauche/droite *sewr lah gaush/dwrat*	on the right/left
tout droit *too dwrah*	straight on
Pour aller à la piscine? *poor allay ah lah piseen*	How do I get to the swimming pool?
la première à gauche *lah prumyair ah gaush*	first on the left
la deuxième à droite *lah duzyem ah dwrat*	second on the right

le marché couvert
luh marshay coovair
indoor market

la zone piétonne _____
lah zohn peeayton
pedestrian zone

Tournez à gauche à la grande place
toornay ah gaush ah lah groñd plas
Turn left at the main square.

3 In conversation (4 minutes)

Il y a un bon restaurant en ville?
eelyah uh boñ restoroñ oñ veel

Is there a good restaurant in town?

Oui, près de la gare.
wee, pray duh lah gar

Yes, near the station.

Pour aller à la gare?
poor allay ah lah gar

How do I get to the station?

4 Words to remember (4 minutes)

Familiarize yourself with these words and test yourself using the cover flap.

traffic lights	**les feux** *lay fuh*
corner	**le coin** *luh kwañ*
street/road	**la rue** *lah roo*
main road	**la rue principale** *lah roo prañseepal*
at the end	**au bout** *oh boo*
map	**la carte** *lah kart*
cross over	**traversez** *travairsay*
opposite	**en face de** *oñ fass duh*

Je me suis perdue.
juh muh swee pairdoo
I'm lost.

le monument
luh moonyumoñ
monument

le plan de la ville
luh plañ duh lah veel
town plan

5 Say it (2 minutes)

Turn right at the end of the street.

It's opposite the town hall.

It's ten minutes by bus.

Tournez à gauche aux feux et puis tout droit.
toornay ah gaush oh fuh ay pwee too dwrah

Turn left at the traffic lights and then straight on.

C'est loin?
say lwañ

Is it far?

Non, c'est cinq minutes à pied.
noñ, say sank minoot ah pyay

No, it's five minutes on foot.

1 Warm up (1 minute)

Say the days of the week in French. (pp.28–9)

How do you say "at six o'clock"? (pp.30–1)

Ask "What time is it?" (pp.30–1)

LE TOURISME
Sightseeing

Most national museums close on Tuesdays and public holidays. Although shops are normally closed on Sundays, in tourist areas many will remain open all weekend. It is not unusual, particularly in rural areas, for shops and public buildings to close at lunch time.

2 Words to remember (4 minutes)

Familiarize yourself with these words and test yourself using the flap.

le guide *luh geed*	guide book
l'entrée (f) *loñtray*	entrance ticket
les heures d'ouverture (f) *lay zur doovairtyur*	opening times
le jour férié *luh joor fairiyay*	public holiday
l'entrée gratuite (f) *loñtray gratweet*	free entrance

la visite guidée
lah viseet geeday
guided tour

Cultural tip The majority of public buildings and private offices close for public holidays. Many public and private offices are closed in August. If a public holiday falls on a Thursday, the French will often **faire le pont** (*do the bridge*) – in other words, take Friday off as well to make a long weekend.

3 In conversation (3 minutes)

Vous ouvrez cet après-midi?
voo zoovray set apray-meedee

Do you open this afternoon?

Oui, mais nous fermons à quatre heures.
wee, may noo fairmoñ ah katruh

Yes, but we close at four o'clock.

Vous avez un accès pour les fauteuils roulants?
voo zavay uñ aksay poor lay fohtuhee roolañ

Do you have wheelchair access?

4 Useful phrases (3 minutes)

Learn these phrases and then test yourself using the cover flap.

What time do you open/close?	**Vous ouvrez/fermez à quelle heure?** *voo zoovray/fairmay ah kel ur*
Where are the toilets?	**Où sont les toilettes?** *oo soñ lay twalet*
Is there wheelchair access?	**Il y a un accès pour les fauteuils roulants?** *eelyah uñ aksay poor lay fohtuhee roolañ*

5 Put into practice (4 minutes)

Cover the text on the right and complete the dialogue in French.

Désolé. Le musée est fermé.
dezolay. luh moozay ay fairmay

Sorry. The museum is closed.

Ask: Do you open on Tuesdays?

Vous ouvrez le mardi?
voo zoovray luh mardee

Oui, mais nous fermons tôt.
wee, may noo fairmoñ toe

Yes, but we close early.

Ask: At what time?

A quelle heure?
ah kel ur

Oui, il y a un ascenseur là-bas.
wee, eelyah uñ asoñsur lah-bah

Yes, there's a lift over there.

Merci, je voudrais quatre entrées.
mairsee, juh voodray katruh oñtray.

Thank you, I'd like four entrance tickets.

Voilà, et le guide est gratuit.
vwalah, ay luh geed ay gratwee

Here you are, and the guidebook is free.

1 Warm up (1 minute)

Say "You're on time".
(pp.14-15)

What's the French for
"ticket"? (pp.38-9)

Say "I am going to
New York". (pp.40-1)

A L'AÉROPORT
At the airport

Although the airport environment is largely universal, it
is sometimes useful to be able to ask your way around
the terminal in French. It's a good idea to make sure
you have a few one-euro coins when you arrive at the
airport; you may need to pay for a baggage trolley.

2 Words to remember (4 minutes)

l'enregistrement (m) *loñrejeestrumoñ*	check-in
le départ *luh depar*	departures
l'arrivée (f) *lareevay*	arrivals
la douane *lah doo-an*	customs
le contrôle des passeports *luh kontrol day passpor*	passport control
le terminal *luh termee-nal*	terminal
la porte d'embarquement *lah port doñbarkumoñ*	gate
le numéro de vol *luh noomairoe duh vol*	flight number

Familiarize yourself with these words
and test yourself using the flap.

**Quelle est la porte d'embarquement pour
le vol numéro vingt-trois?**
*kel ay lah port doñbarkumoñ poor luh vol
numairoh vañ-trwah*
What gate does flight 23 leave from?

3 Useful phrases (3 minutes)

Learn these phrases and then test yourself
using the cover flap.

Le vol pour Nice est à l'heure? *luh vol poor nees et ah lur*	Is the flight for Nice on time?

| **Je ne trouve pas mes bagages.** *juh nuh troov pah may bagarj* | I can't find my baggage. |

| **Le vol pour Londres est retardé.** *luh vol poor londruh ay retarday* | The flight to London is delayed. |

4 Put into practice (3 minutes)

Join in this conversation. Read the French on the left and follow the instructions to make your reply. Then test yourself by concealing the answers with the cover flap.

Bonsoir, monsieur. Je peux vous aider?
boñswar, musyuh. juh puh voo zayday

Good evening, sir. Can I help you?

Ask: Is the flight to Paris on time?

Le vol pour Paris est à l'heure?
luh vol poor paree et ah lur

Oui, monsieur
wee musyuh

Yes, sir.

Ask: What gate does it leave from?

Quelle est la porte d'embarquement?
kel ay lah port doñbarkumoñ

5 Match and repeat (4 minutes)

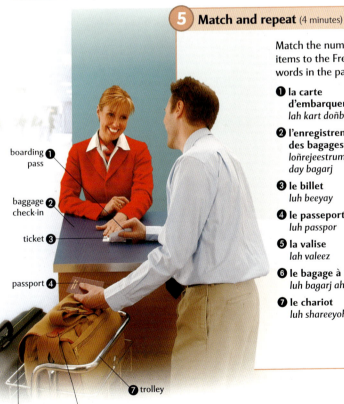

Match the numbered items to the French words in the panel.

❶ la carte d'embarquement
lah kart doñbarkumoñ

❷ l'enregistrement des bagages (m)
loñrejeestrumoñ day bagarj

❸ le billet
luh beeyay

❹ le passeport
luh passpor

❺ la valise
lah valeez

❻ le bagage à main
luh bagarj ah mañ

❼ le chariot
luh shareeyoh

boarding ❶ pass

baggage ❷ check-in

ticket ❸

passport ❹

❺ suitcase   ❻ hand luggage   ❼ trolley

RÉVISEZ ET RÉPÉTEZ
Review and repeat

1 Places

❶ **le musée**
luh moozay

❷ **la mairie**
lah mayree

❸ **le pont**
luh poñ

❹ **la galerie d'art**
lah galree dar

❺ **le parking**
luh parking

❻ **la cathédrale**
lah kataydral

❼ **la place**
lah plas

1 Places (4 minutes)

Name the numbered places in French.

❶ museum ❷ town hall ❸ bridge

❹ art gallery ❺ car park

❻ cathedral

❼ square

2 Car parts

❶ **le pare-brise**
luh parbreez

❷ **le clignotant**
luh kleenyoe-toñ

❸ **le capot**
luh kapoh

❹ **le pneu**
luh pnuh

❺ **la portière**
lah portyair

❻ **le pare-chocs**
luh parshok

2 Car parts (3 minutes)

Name these car parts in French.

windscreen ❶

❹ tyre ❺ door

3 Questions (4 minutes)

Ask the questions that match these answers.

❶ **Le car part à huit heures.**
luh kar par ah weet ur

❷ **Le café, c'est deux euros cinquante.**
luh kafay, say duh zuroh sankont

❸ **Non, je ne veux pas de vin.**
noñ. juh nuh vuh pah duh vañ

❹ **Le train part du quai cinq.**
luh trañ par doo kay sank

❺ **Nous allons à Paris.**
noo zalloñ ah paree

❻ **Non, c'est cinq minutes à pied.**
noñ, say sank minoot ah pyay

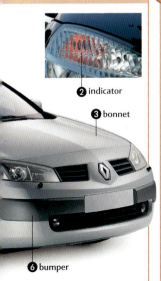

3 Questions

❶ **Le car part à quelle heure?**
luh kar par ah kel ur

❷ **C'est combien le café?**
say koñbyañ luh kafay

❸ **Vous voulez du vin?**
voo voolay doo vañ

❹ **Le train part de quel quai?**
luh trañ par duh kel kay

❺ **Où allez-vous?**
oo allay voo

❻ **C'est loin?**
say lwañ

❷ indicator

❸ bonnet

❻ bumper

4 Verbs (4 minutes)

Choose the correct words to fill the gaps.

❶ **Je _____ anglais.**

❷ **Nous _____ le bus.**

❸ **Elle _____ à Paris.**

❹ **Il _____ trois filles.**

❺ **Tu _____ un thé?**

❻ **Combien d'enfants _____ -vous?**

❼ **Je _____ rendez-vous pour mardi.**

❽ **Où _____ les toilettes?**

4 Verbs

❶ **suis**
swee

❷ **prenons**
prunoñ

❸ **va**
vah

❹ **a**
ah

❺ **veux**
vuh

❻ **avez**
avay

❼ **prends**
proñ

❽ **sont**
soñ

1 Warm up (1 minute)

How do you ask in French "Do you accept credit cards?" (pp.38-9)

Ask "How much is that?" (pp.18-19)

Ask "Do you have children?" (pp.12-13)

RÉSERVER LES CHAMBRES
Booking a room

There are different types of accommodation: **l'hôtel,** categorized from one to five stars; **la pension,** a small family-run hotel; and **les chambres d'hôte** (like bed and breakfast) which are often situated in beautiful old properties.

2 Useful phrases (3 minutes)

Practise these phrases and then test yourself by concealing the French on the left with the cover flap.

Le petit-déjeuner est compris?
luh puhtee dayjunay ay koñpree

Is breakfast included?

Vous acceptez les animaux de compagnie?
voo zakseptay lay zanimoe duh koñpañee

Do you accept pets?

Vous avez un room service?
voo zavay uñ room survees

Do you have room service?

Il faut libérer la chambre à quelle heure?
eel foe leeburay lah shombruh ah kel ur

What time do I have to vacate the room?

3 In conversation (5 minutes)

Vous avez des chambres libres?
voo zavay day shombruh leebruh

Do you have any vacancies?

Oui, une chambre double.
wee, oon shombruh doobluh

Yes, a double room.

Vous avez un lit d'enfant?
voo zavay uñ lee doñfoñ

Do you have a cot?

4 Words to remember (4 minutes)

Familiarize yourself with these words and test yourself by concealing the French on the right with the cover flap.

room	**la chambre** *lah shombruh*
single room	**la chambre simple** *lah shombruh sampluh*
double room	**la chambre double** *lah shombruh doobluh*
twin room	**la chambre twin** *lah shombruh twin*
bathroom	**la salle de bains** *lah sal duh bañ*
shower	**la douche** *lah doosh*
breakfast	**le petit-déjeuner** *luh puhtee dayjunay*
key	**la clé** *lah klay*
balcony	**le balcon** *luh balkoñ*
air-conditioning	**la climatisation** *lah kleematee-zasyoñ*

La chambre donne sur le jardin?
lah shombruh don syur luh jardañ
Does the room have a view over the garden?

5 Say it (2 minutes)

Do you have a single room?

Does the room have a balcony?

Cultural tip Chambres d'hôte are usually the only type of accommodation to include breakfast in the price of the room. In other types of hotel you will usually be charged extra. Many two- or three-star hotels belong to the Logis de France association, which guarantees standards of accommodation and service.

Pas de problème. Combien de nuits?
pah duh prob-lem. koñbyañ duh nwee

No problem. How many nights?

Pour trois nuits.
poor trwah nwee

For three nights.

Très bien. Voici la clé.
tray byañ. vwasee lah klay

Very good. Here's the key.

1 **Warm up** (1 minute)

How do you say "is there...?" and "there isn't..."? (pp.48–9)

What does "Je peux vous aider?" mean? (pp.48–9)

A L'HÔTEL
In the hotel

Although the larger hotels almost always have bathrooms en suite, there are still some **pensions** and **chambres d'hôte** with shared facilities. This can also be the case in some economy hotels, where a whole family can stay the night for less than the price of a tank of petrol.

2 **Match and repeat** (6 minutes)

Match the numbered items in this hotel bedroom with the French text in the panel and test yourself using the cover flap.

❶ **la table de chevet**
lah tabluh duh shuvay

❷ **la lampe**
lah lomp

❸ **le minibar**
luh meeneebar

❹ **les rideaux** (m)
lay reedoe

❺ **le canapé**
luh kanapay

❻ **l'oreiller** (m)
lorayay

❼ **le coussin**
luh koosañ

❽ **le lit**
luh lee

❾ **le dessus de lit**
luh dusoo duh lee

❿ **la couverture**
lah coovurtyur

curtains ❹

bedside table ❶

sofa ❺

❸ minibar

lamp ❷

❽ bed

bedspread ❾

blanket ❿

❻ pillow   ❼ cushion

Cultural tip When you arrive in your room, you will usually see a long sausage-shaped pillow on the bed called **le traversin** - nowadays a largely decorative item. These are hard and not very comfortable. However, you can usually find square, softer pillows (**les oreillers**) in the cupboard. Do not hesitate to ask if you can't find any.

3 Useful phrases (5 minutes)

Familiarize yourself with these phrases and then test yourself.

The room is too cold/hot.	**La chambre est trop froide/chaude.** *lah shombruh ay troe fwrard/shohd*

There are no towels.	**Il n'y a pas de serviettes.** *eenyah pah duh survyet*

I need some soap.	**J'ai besoin de savon.** *jay buzwañ duh savoñ*

The shower doesn't work very well.	**La douche ne marche pas très bien.** *lah doosh nuh marsh pah tray byañ*

The lift has broken down.	**L'ascenseur est en panne.** *lasohsur ay toñ pan*

4 Put into practice (3 minutes)

Cover the text on the right and complete the dialogue in French.

Je peux vous aider? **J'ai besoin d'oreillers.**
juh puh voo zayday *jay buzwañ dorayay*

Can I help you?

Say: I need some pillows.

La femme de chambre va les apporter. **Et la télévision ne marche pas.**
la fam duh shambruh vah lay zaportay *ay lah telayveesyoñ nuh marsh pah*

The maid will bring some.

Say: And the television doesn't work.

1 **Warm up** (1 minute)

Ask "Can I?" (pp.34-5)

What is French for "the shower"? (pp.60-1)

Say "I need some towels". (pp.60-1)

AU CAMPING
At the campsite

Camping is popular in France and there are many well-organized campsites. These are rated by a star system. Most towns have **un camping municipal** (*public campsite*), and there are also many private sites. Campfires are usually forbidden, but you can often hire a barbecue.

2 **Useful phrases** (3 minutes)

Familiarize yourself with these phrases and then test yourself using the cover flap.

Je peux louer un vélo? *juh puh looway uñ vayloe*	Can I rent a bicycle?
C'est de l'eau potable? *say duh loe potabluh*	Is this drinking water?
Les feux de camp sont permis? *lay fuh duh koñ soñ pairmee*	Are campfires allowed?
Les radios sont interdites. *lay radyo soñ añtairdeet*	Radios are forbidden.

Le camping est tranquille
luh komping ay troñkeel
The campsite is quiet.

le bureau du camping
luh buroh doo komping
campsite office

la poubelle
lah poobel
litter bin

le double toit
luh doobluh twah
fly sheet

3 **In conversation:** (5 minutes)

J'ai besoin d'un emplacement pour trois nuits.
jay buzwañ d'uñ oñplasmoñ poor trwah nwee

I need a pitch for three nights.

Il y en a un près de la piscine.
eelyon ah uñ pray duh lah piseen

There's one near the swimming pool.

C'est combien pour une caravane?
say koñbyañ poor oon karavan

How much is it for a caravan?

5 Say it (2 minutes)

I need a pitch for four nights.

Can I rent a tent?

Where's the electrical hook-up?

4 Words to remember (4 minutes)

Familiarize yourself with these words and test yourself using the cover flap.

tent	**la tente**	*lah tont*
caravan	**la caravane**	*lah karavan*
camper van	**le camping-car**	*luh komping-car*
campsite	**le camping**	*luh komping*
pitch	**l'emplacement** (m)	*loñplasmoñ*
campfire	**le feu de camp**	*luh fuh duh koñ*
drinking water	**l'eau potable** (f)	*loe potabluh*
rubbish	**les détritus** (m)	*lay daytreetoo*
showers	**les douches** (f)	*lay doosh*
camping gas	**le camping-gaz**	*luh komping-gaz*
sleeping bag	**le sac de couchage**	*luh sak duh koosharj*
air mattress	**le matelas pneumatique**	*luh mataylah nyumateek*
ground sheet	**le tapis de sol**	*luh tapee duh sol*

les toilettes (f)
lay twalet
toilets

le branchement électrique
luh bronshmoñ aylektreek
electrical hook-up

la corde
lah kord
guy rope

le piquet
luh peekay
tent peg

Cinquante euros, avec une nuit d'avance.
sankoñt uroh, avek oon nwee davons

Fifty euros, one night in advance.

Je peux louer un barbecue?
juh puh looway uñ barbekyoo

Can I rent a barbecue?

Oui, mais vous devez verser des arrhes.
wee, may voo duvay vairsay day zar

Yes, but you must pay a deposit.

1 **Warm up** (1 minute)

Say "hot" and "cold".
(pp.60-1)

What is the French for
"bathroom" (pp.58-9),
"bed", and "pillow"?
(pp.60-1)

LES DESCRIPTIONS
Descriptions

Adjectives are words used to describe people, things,
and places. In French you generally put the adjective
after the thing it describes - for example, **une
chambre froide** (*a cold room*), but in some cases
the adjective is placed before - for example, **un grand
café** (*a large coffee*).

2 **Words to remember** (7 minutes)

Adjectives can change slightly depending on whether the
thing described is masculine (**le**), feminine (**la**), or plural (**les**),
but often this affects only the spelling, not the pronunciation.
Below, the masculine spelling is followed by the feminine.
For the plural form, just add a (silent) "s" to the appropriate
masculine or feminine form.

grand/grande *groñ/groñd*	big/tall
petit/petite *puhtee/puhteet*	small
chaud/chaude *shoh/shohd*	hot
froid/froide *fwrah/fwrad*	cold
bon/bonne *boñ/bon*	good
mauvais/mauvaise *movay/movez*	bad
lent/lente *loñ/lont*	slow
rapide/rapide *rapeed/rapeed*	fast
bruyant/bruyante *breeyoñ/breeyont*	noisy
tranquille/tranquille *troñkeel/troñkeel*	quiet
dur/dure *dyuh/dyuh*	hard
mou/molle *moo/moll*	soft
beau/belle *boe/bell*	beautiful
laid/laide *leh/led*	ugly

la haute montagne
lah oht moñtanhyuh
high mountain

la basse colline
lah bas koleen
low hill

la petite maison
lah puhteet mayzon
small house

la vieille église
lah veeyay egleez
old church

**Le village est
très beau.**
luh veelarj ay tray boe
The village is
very beautiful.

3 Useful phrases (4 minutes)

You can emphasize a description by using **très** (*very*),
trop (*too*), or **plus** (*more*) before the adjective.

This coffee is cold.	**Ce café est froid.** *suh kafay ay fwrah*
My room is very noisy.	**Ma chambre est très bruyante.** *mah shombruh ay tray breeyont*
My car is too small.	**Ma voiture est trop petite.** *mah vwatyur ay troe puhteet*
I need a softer bed.	**J'ai besoin d'un lit plus mou.** *jay buzwañ d'uñ lee ploo moo*

4 Put into practice (3 minutes)

Join in this conversation. Cover up the text on the right and complete the dialogue
in French. Check and repeat if necessary.

Voici la chambre. *vwasee lah shombruh* Here is the bedroom. Say: The view is very beautiful.	**La vue est très belle.** *lah voo ay tray bell*
La salle de bains est là-bas. *luh sal duh bañ ay lah-bah* The bathroom is over there. Say: It is too small.	**Elle est trop petite.** *el ay troe puhteet*
Nous n'en avons pas d'autre. *noo nañavoñ pah dotruh* We haven't got another. Say: Then we'll take the room.	**Alors nous prenons la chambre.** *Alor noo prunoñ lah shombruh*

Réponses
Answers (Cover with flap)

RÉVISEZ ET RÉPÉTEZ
Review and repeat

1 Adjectives

❶ **chaude**
shohd

❷ **mou**
moo

❸ **bon**
boñ

❹ **petite**
puhteet

❺ **tranquille**
troñkeel

1 Adjectives (3 minutes)

Put the adjective in brackets into French, using the correct masculine or feminine form.

❶ La chambre est trop _____ . (hot)

❷ Je voudrais un oreiller plus _____ . (soft)

❸ Le café est _____ . (good)

❹ Cette salle de bains est trop _____ . (small)

❺ Vous avez une chambre plus _____ ? (quiet)

2 Campsite

❶ **le branchement électrique**
luh bronshmoñ aylektreek

❷ **la tente**
lah tont

❸ **la poubelle**
lah poobel

❹ **la corde**
lah kord

❺ **les toilettes**
lay twalet

❻ **la caravane**
lah karavan

2 Campsite (3 minutes)

Name these items you might find in a campsite.

tent ❷   guy rope ❹

electrical ❶
hook-up

litter bin ❸

3 At the hotel (4 minutes)

You are booking a room in a hotel. Follow the conversation, replying in French by following the English prompts.

Je peux vous aider?
❶ Do you have any vacancies?

Oui, une chambre double.
❷ Do you accept pets?

Oui. C'est pour combien de nuits?
❸ Three nights.

Ça fait deux cent quarante euros.
❹ Is breakfast included?

Bien sûr, voici la clé.
❺ Thank you very much.

3 At the hotel

❶ **Vous avez des chambres libres?**
voo zavay day shombruh leebruh

❷ **Vous acceptez les animaux de compagnie?**
voo zakseptay lay zanimoe duh koñpañee

❸ **Trois nuits.**
trwah nwee

❹ **Le petit-déjeuner est compris?**
luh puhtee dayjuhnay ay koñpree

❺ **Merci beaucoup.**
mairsee bohkoo

4 Negatives (5 minutes)

Make these sentences negative using the verb in brackets.

❶ Je _____ d'enfants.
(avoir)

❷ Elle _____ à Paris demain.
(aller)

❸ Il _____ de vin.
(vouloir)

❹ Je _____ le train pour Nice.
(prendre)

❺ Le café _____ chaud. (être)

4 Negatives

❶ **n'ai pas**
nay pah

❷ **ne va pas**
nuh vah pah

❸ **ne veut pas**
nuh vuh pah

❹ **ne prends pas**
nuh proñ pah

❺ **n'est pas**
nay pah

❺ toilets

❻ caravan

1 **Warm up** (1 minute)

Ask "How do I get to the station?" (pp.50-1)

Say "Turn left at the traffic lights", "Cross over the street", "The station is opposite the café". (pp.50-1)

LES MAGASINS
Shops

In town centres, shops (**magasins**) are often traditional, specialist outlets. But you can also find big supermarkets and shopping malls on the outskirts of major towns. Local markets selling fresh, local produce can be found everywhere. You can find out the market day at the tourist office.

2 **Match and repeat** (5 minutes)

Match the numbered shops below and right to the French in the panel. Then test yourself using the cover flap.

❶ **la boulangerie**
lah booloñjuree

❷ **la pâtisserie**
lah pateesree

❸ **le tabac**
luh tabah

❹ **la boucherie**
lah boosheree

❺ **la charcuterie**
lah sharkooterie

❻ **la librairie**
lah leebrairee

❼ **la poissonnerie**
lah pwasoñree

❽ **l'épicerie** (m)
laypeesree

❾ **la banque**
lah boñk

❶ baker

❷ cake shop

❹ butcher

❺ delicatessen

❼ fishmonger

❽ grocer

Cultural tip As well as supplying medicines and health products, a French pharmacy (**pharmacie**) will sell expensive perfume and cosmetics but not generally an everyday bar of soap or a tube of toothpaste. The latter are found at the supermarket or general store. The **tabac** (*tobacconist*) is the place for newspapers and stamps, but also often incorporates a café and bar.

Où est la fleuriste?
oo ay lah flureest
Where is the florist?

❸ tobacconist

❻ bookshop

❾ bank

---

3 Words to remember (4 minutes)

Familiarize yourself with these words and test yourself using the flap.

hardware shop	**la quincaillerie** *lah kañkayeree*
antique shop	**l'antiquaire** (m) *lañteekair*
hairdresser	**le coiffeur** *luh kwafur*
jeweller	**la bijouterie** *lah bee-jooteree*
post office	**la poste** *lah post*
shoemaker	**la cordonnerie** *lah kordoneree*
dry cleaner	**le pressing** *luh praysing*
confectioner	**le confiseur** *luh koñfeesur*
cheese shop	**la fromagerie** *lah fromajeree*

---

4 Useful phrases (3 minutes)

Familiarize yourself with these phrases.

Where is the hairdresser?	**Où est le coiffeur?** *oo ay luh kwafur*
Where do I pay?	**Je dois payer où?** *juh dwah payay oo*
I'm just looking, thank you.	**Je regarde, merci.** *juh rugard, mairsee*
Do you sell SIM cards?	**Vous vendez des cartes SIM?** *voo vonday day kart seem*
I'd like two of these.	**J'en veux deux.** *joñ vuh duh*
Is there a department store in town?	**Il y a un grand magasin en ville?** *eelyah uñ groñ magazañ oñ veel*
Can I place an order?	**Je peux passer une commande?** *juh puh passay oon komond*

---

5 Say it (2 minutes)

Where is the bank?

Do you sell cheese?

Where do I pay?

1 **Warm up** (1 minute)

What is French for 40, 56, 77, 82, and 94? (pp.30-1)

Say "I'd like a big room". (pp.64-5)

Ask "Do you have a small car?" (pp.64-5)

AU MARCHÉ
At the market

France uses the metric system of weights and measures. You need to ask for produce in kilogrammes or grammes. You may find that the older generation still use the term **une livre** (*a pound*) meaning half a kilo. Some larger items such as melons are sold individually **à la pièce**.

2 **Match and repeat** (4 minutes)

Match the numbered items in this scene with the text in the panel.

❶ **les courgettes** (f)
lay korjet

❷ **la salade**
lah sah-lad

❸ **les citrons** (m)
lay sitroñ

❹ **les poireaux** (m)
lay pwaroe

❺ **les tomates** (f)
lay toemat

❻ **les champignons** (m)
lay shoñpeeyoñ

❼ **les avocats** (m)
lay zavokah

❽ **les pommes de terre** (f)
lay pom duh tair

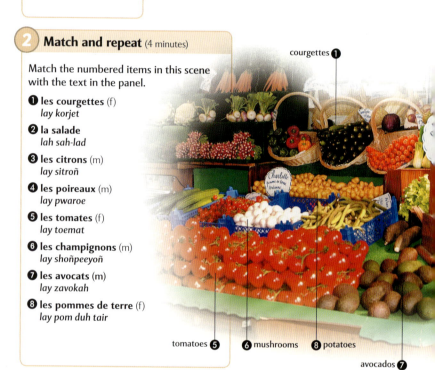

courgettes ❶

tomatoes ❺   ❻ mushrooms   ❽ potatoes

avocados ❼

3 **In conversation** (3 minutes)

Je voudrais des tomates.
juh voodray day toemat

I'd like some tomatoes.

Des grosses ou des petites?
day gros oo day puhteet

The large ones or the small ones?

Deux kilos de grosse, s'il vous plaît.
duh keeloe duh gros, seel voo play

Two kilos of the large ones, please.

Cultural tip France now uses the common European currency, the euro. This is divided into 100 cents, which the French call **centimes** after the old divisions of the franc. You will usually hear the price given as: **dix euros, vingt** (€10.20), **six euros, soixante-treize** (€6.73), etc.

② lettuce

③ lemons

④ leeks

4 Useful phrases (5 minutes)

Learn these phrases. Then cover up the answers on the right. Read the English under the pictures and say the phrase in French as shown on the right.

Le fromage de chèvre est trop cher.
luh fromarj duh shevruh ay troe shair

The goat's cheese is too expensive.

C'est combien ce fromage?
say koñbyañ suh fromarj

How much is that cheese?

Ce sera tout.
suh surah too

That'll be all.

5 Say it (2 minutes)

Three kilos of potatoes, please.

The mushrooms are too expensive.

How much is the lettuce?

Et avec ceci, madame.
ay avek susee, ma-dam

Anything else, madam.

Ce sera tout, merci. C'est combien?
suh surah too, mairsee. say koñbyañ

That'll be all, thank you. How much?

Trois euros, cinquante.
trwah zuroh, sankont

Three euros, fifty.

AU SUPERMARCHÉ
At the supermarket

1 **Warm up** (1 minute)

What are these items
you could buy in a
supermarket (pp.24-5)?

la viande
le poisson
le fromage
le jus de fruits
le vin
l'eau

Prices in supermarkets are usually lower than in smaller
shops. They offer all kinds of products, with the larger
out-of-town **hypermarchés** (*hypermarkets*) extending
to clothes, household goods, garden furniture, and DIY
products. They may also stock regional products.

2 **Match and repeat** (5 minutes)

Look at the numbered items and match
them to the French words in the panel
on the left.

❶ les produits d'entretien (m)
lay prodwee doñtruh-tiañ

❷ les fruits (m)
lay froo-wee

❸ les boissons (m)
lay bwassoñ

❹ les plats préparés (m)
lay plah prayparay

❺ les légumes (m)
lay laygoom

❻ les produits surgelés (m)
lay prodwee surjulay

❼ les produits laitiers (m)
lay prodwee letyay

❽ les produits de beauté (m)
lay prodwee duh boetay

household ❶ products

fruit ❷

drinks ❸

ready meals ❹

vegetables ❺

frozen foods ❻

Cultural tip Fruit and vegetables sold by the kilo are usually
weighed and priced at a separate counter. Alternatively, there
may sometimes be a self-service weighing machine.

3 Useful phrases (3 minutes)

Learn these phrases and then test yourself using the cover flap.

May I have a bag, please?	**Je peux avoir un sac, s'il vous plaît?** *juh puh avwar uñ sak, seel voo play*
Where is the drinks aisle?	**Où est le rayon des boissons?** *oo ay luh rayonn day bwassoñ*
Where is the check-out, please?	**Où est la caisse, s'il vous plaît?** *oo ay lah kes, seel voo play*
Please key in your PIN.	**Tapez votre code, s'il vous plaît.** *tapay votruh kod, seel voo play*

❽ beauty products

❼ dairy products

4 Words to remember (4 minutes)

Learn these words and then test yourself using the cover flap.

bread	**le pain** *luh pañ*
milk	**le lait** *luh lay*
butter	**le beurre** *luh bur*
ham	**le jambon** *luh joñboñ*
salt	**le sel** *luh sel*
pepper	**le poivre** *luh pwavruh*
washing powder	**la lessive** *lah leseev*
toilet paper	**le papier toilette** *luh papyay twalet*
nappies	**les couches** (f) *lay koosh*
washing-up liquid	**le liquide vaisselle** *luh likeed vaysel*

5 Say it (2 minutes)

Where's the dairy products aisle?

May I have some ham, please?

Where are the frozen foods?

VÊTEMENTS ET CHAUSSURES
Clothes and shoes

1 Warm up (1 minute)

Say "I'd like...". (pp.22-3)

Ask "Do you have...? (pp.14-5)

Say "38", "42", and "46". (pp.30-1)

Say "large", "small", "bigger", and "smaller". (pp.64-5)

Clothes and shoes are measured in metric sizes. Even allowing for conversion of sizes, French clothes tend to be cut smaller than English ones. Note that clothes size is **la taille** but shoe size is **la pointure**.

2 Match and repeat (3 minutes)

Match the numbered items of clothing to the French words in the panel on the left. Use the cover flap to test yourself.

❶ **la chemise**
lah shumeez

❷ **la cravate**
lah kravat

❸ **la veste**
lah vest

❹ **la poche**
lah posh

❺ **la manche**
lah moñsh

❻ **le pantalon**
luh poñtaloñ

❼ **la jupe**
lah joop

❽ **le collants** (m)
luh kolloñ

❾ **les chaussures** (f)
lay shohsyur

shirt ❶

tie ❷

jacket ❸

pocket ❹

sleeve ❺

trousers ❻

Cultural tip Like most of Europe, France uses the continental system of sizes. Dress sizes usually range from 36 (UK 8, US 6) through to 46 (UK 20, US 18) and shoe sizes from 37 (UK 4½, US 6) to 45 (UK 11, US 12). For men's shirts, a size 41 is a 16-inch collar, 43 is a 17-inch collar, and 45 is an 18-inch collar.

3 **Useful phrases** (5 minutes)

Learn these phrases and then test yourself using the cover flap.

| Do you have a larger size? | **Vous avez une taille plus grande?** |
| | *voo zavay oon tie ploo groñd* |

| It's not what I want. | **Ce n'est pas ce que je veux.** |
| | *suh nay pah sukuh juh vuh* |

| I'll take the pink one. | **Je prends la rose.** |
| | *juh proñ lah roz* |

4 **Words to remember** (4 minutes)

Colours are adjectives (pp.64–5) and often have a masculine, feminine, and plural form. The feminine is usually formed by adding an **e** and the plural by adding an **s**.

red	**rouge/rouge**
	rooj/rooj
white	**blanc/blanche**
	bloñ/blonsh
blue	**bleu/bleue**
	bluh/bluh
yellow	**jaune/jaune**
	jon/jon
green	**vert/verte**
	vair/vairt
black	**noir/noire**
	nwar/nwar

7 skirt

8 tights

9 shoes

5 **Say it** (2 minutes)

I'll take the yellow one.

Do you have this jacket in black?

I'd like a 38.

Do you have a smaller size?

RÉVISEZ ET RÉPÉTEZ
Review and repeat

① Market

❶ les tomates
lay toemat

❷ les champignons
lay shoñpeeyoñ

❸ les pommes de terre
lay pom duh tair

❹ les courgettes
lay korjet

❺ la salade
lah sah-lad

❻ les avocats
lay zavokah

① Market (3 minutes)

Name the numbered vegetables in French.

❶ tomatoes
❷ mushrooms
❸ potatoes
❹ courgettes
❺ lettuce
❻ avocados

② Description

❶ These shoes are too expensive.
❷ My room is very small.
❸ I need a softer bed.

② Description (2 minutes)

What do these sentences mean?

❶ Ces chaussures sont trop chères.
❷ Ma chambre est très petite.
❸ J'ai besoin d'un lit plus mou.

③ Shops

❶ la boulangerie
lah booloñjuree

❷ l'épicerie
laypeesree

❸ la librairie
lah leebrairee

❹ la poissonnerie
lah pwasoñree

❺ la pâtisserie
lah pateesree

❻ la boucherie
lah boosheree

③ Shops (3 minutes)

Name the numbered shops in French then check your answers.

❶ baker ❷ grocer ❸ bookshop

❹ fishmonger ❺ cake shop ❻ butcher

4 Supermarket (3 minutes)

What is the French for the numbered product categories?

❶ household products
❷ beauty products
❸ drinks
❹ dairy products
❺ frozen foods

4 Supermarket

❶ **les produits d'entretien**
lay prodwee doñtruh-tiañ

❷ **les produits de beauté**
lay prodwee duh boetay

❸ **les boissons**
lay bwassoñ

❹ **les produits laitiers**
lay prodwee letyay

❺ **les produits surgelés**
lay prodwee surjulay

5 Museum (4 minutes)

Follow this conversation replying in French following the English prompts.

Bonjour. Je peux vous aider?
❶ Three adults and two children.

Ça fait soixante-dix euros.
❷ That's very expensive!

Nous ne faisons pas de réductions pour les enfants.
❸ How much is a guide?

Quinze euros.
❹ Five tickets and a guide, please.

Quatre-vingt-cinq euros, s'il vous plaît.
❺ Here you are. Where are the toilets?

Là-bas.
❻ Thank you very much.

5 Museum

❶ **Trois adultes et deux enfants.**
trwah zadoolt ay duh zoñfoñ

❷ **C'est très cher!**
say tray shair

❸ **C'est combien pour un guide?**
say koñbyañ poor uñ geed

❹ **Cinq entrées et un guide, s'il vous plaît**
sank oñtray ay tuñ geed, seel voo play

❺ **Voilà. Où sont les toilettes?**
vwalah. oo soñ lay twalet

❻ **Merci beaucoup.**
mairsee bohkoo

1 **Warm up** (1 minute)

Ask "which platform?"
(pp.38-9)

What is the French for
the following family
members: "sister",
"brother", "mother",
"father", "son", and
"daughter"? (pp.10-11)

OCCUPATIONS
Jobs

Some occupations have a different form when the
person is female - for example, **infirmier** (*male nurse*)
and **infirmière** (*female nurse*). Others such as
professeur remain the same for men and women.
When you say your occupation, you don't use
un/une (*a*); as in **Je suis avocat** (*I'm a lawyer*).

2 **Words to remember: jobs** (7 minutes)

Familiarize yourself with these occupations and test
yourself using the flap. The feminine form is shown
in parentheses.

médecin *medsañ*	doctor
dentiste *doñteest*	dentist
infirmier(ière) *añfairmyay(yair)*	nurse
professeur *profesur*	teacher
comptable *koñtabluh*	accountant
avocat(e) *avokah(aht)*	lawyer
designer *deesienur*	designer
consultant(e) *koñsooltoñ(oñt)*	consultant
secrétaire *sekraytair*	secretary
commerçant(e) *komairsoñ(oñt)*	shopkeeper
électricien(ne) *aylektreesyañ(en)*	electrician
plombier *ploñbyay*	plumber
cuisinier(ière) *kweeseenyay(yair)*	cook/chef
ingénieur *añjaynyur*	engineer
à mon compte *ah moñ kont*	self-employed

Je suis plombier.
juh swee ploñbyay
I'm a plumber.

Elle est professeur.
el ay profesur
She is a teacher.

3 Put into practice (4 minutes)

Join in the conversation. Conceal the text on the right with the cover flap and complete the dialogue in French.

Quelle est votre profession?
kel ay votruh profesyoñ

What do you do?

Say: I am a consultant.

Je suis consultant.
juh swee koñsooltoñ

Vous travaillez pour quelle compagnie?
voo trav-eyeyay poor kel koñpanee

What company do you work for?

Say: I'm self-employed.

Je suis à mon compte.
juh swee ah moñ kont

Comme c'est intéressant!
kom say añtayraysoñ

How interesting!

Ask: What is your profession?

Et quelle est votre profession?
ay kel ay votruh profesyoñ

Je suis dentiste.
juh swee doñteest

I'm a dentist.

Say: My sister is a dentist too.

Ma sœur est dentiste aussi.
mah sur ay doñteest ohsee

---

4 Words to remember: workplace (3 minutes)

Familiarize yourself with these words and test yourself.

head office	**le siège social** *luh syej sosyal*
branch	**lah succursale** *lah sookoorsal*
department	**le département** *luh daypartumoñ*
reception	**la réception** *lah resepsyoñ*
manager	**le chef** *luh shef*
trainee	**le stagiaire** *luh stajyair*

Le siège social est à Lille.
lluh syej sosyal ay tah leel
Head office is in Lille.

LE BUREAU
The office

1 **Warm up** (1 minute)

Practise different ways of introducing yourself in different situations (pp.8–9). Mention your name, occupation, nationality, and any other information you'd like to volunteer.

An office environment or business situation has its own vocabulary in any language, but there are many items for which the terminology is virtually universal. Be aware that French computer keyboards have a different layout to the standard English QWERTY convention.

2 **Words to remember** (5 minutes)

Familiarize yourself with these words. Read them aloud several times and try to memorize them. Conceal the French with the cover flap and test yourself.

le moniteur *luh moneetur*	monitor
l'ordinateur (m) *lordeenatur*	computer
la souris *lah sooree*	mouse
l'email (m) *leemail*	e-mail
l'internet (m) *lañtairnet*	internet
le mot de passe *luh moh duh pas*	password
la messagerie **téléphonique** *lah mesah-juree telayfoneek*	voicemail
le code wifi *luh kod weefee*	Wi-Fi code
le copieur *luh kopee-ur*	photocopier
l'agenda (m) *lajeñdah*	diary
la carte de visite *lah kart duh veezeet*	business card
la réunion *lah rayoonyon*	meeting
la conférence *lah konfayroñs*	conference
l'ordre du jour (m) *lordruh doo joor*	agenda

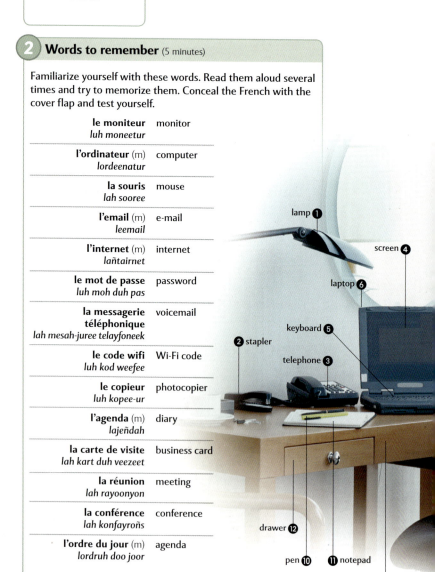

lamp **1**

screen **4**

laptop **6**

keyboard **5**

2 stapler

telephone **3**

drawer **12**

pen **10**   **11** notepad

7 desk

3 Useful phrases (2 minutes)

Learn these phrases and then test yourself using the cover flap.

I need to make some photocopies. | **J'ai besoin de faire des photocopies.**
jay buzwañ duh fair day fotokopee

I'd like to arrange an appointment. | **Je voudrais prendre rendez-vous.**
juh voodray proñdruh roñday-voo

I want to send an e-mail. | **Je veux envoyer un email.**
juh vuh oñvwayay uñ eemail

4 Match and repeat (5 minutes)

Match the numbered items to the French words on the right.

5 Say it (2 minutes)

I'd like to arrange a conference.

Do you have a business card?

I have a laptop.

clock **8**

printer **9**

13 swivel chair

❶ **la lampe**
lah lomp

❷ **l'agrafeuse** (f)
lagrafurz

❸ **le téléphone**
luh telayfon

❹ **l'écran** (m)
laykroñ

❺ **le clavier**
luh klaveeyay

❻ **l'ordinateur portable** (m)
lordeenatur portabluh

❼ **le bureau**
luh byuroh

❽ **la pendule**
lah poñdool

❾ **l'imprimante** (f)
lampreemont

❿ **le stylo**
el luh steeloh

⓫ **le bloc-notes**
eluh blok-not

⓬ **le tiroir**
luh teerwar

⓭ **la chaise tournante**
lah shayz toornont

1 Warm up (1 minute)

Say "How interesting!"
(p.78-9), "library"
(pp.48-9), and "traffic
lights". (pp.50-1)

Ask "What is your
profession?" and answer
"I'm an engineer".
(pp.78-9)

LE MONDE ACADÉMIQUE
Academic world

In France **une licence** (*batchelor's degree*)
generally takes three years, followed by **une
maîtrise** (*master's degree*) and **un doctorat**
(*PhD*). Paris has several universities, often
referred to by Roman numerals, as in Paris V.

2 Useful phrases (3 minutes)

Familiarize yourself with these phrases
and then test yourself.

Quel est votre secteur? *kel ay votruh sektur*	What is your field?
Je fais de la recherche en chimie. *juh fay duh lah reshairsh oñ sheemee*	I am doing research in chemistry.
J'ai une licence en droit. *jay oon leesons oñ dwrah*	I have a degree in law.
Je fais une présentation sur l'architecture moderne. *juh fay oon praysoñtasyoñ syur larsheetektur modairn*	I am giving a presentation on modern architecture.

3 In conversation (5 minutes)

**Bonjour, je suis
professeur Stein.**
*boñjoor, juh swee profesur
stayeen*

Hello, I'm Professor
Stein.

**De quelle université
êtes-vous?**
*duh kel ooneevair-sitay et
voo*

What university are
you from?

**Je suis déléguée de
l'université Paris II.**
*juh swee daylaygay duh
looneevair-sitay paree duh*

I'm the delegate from
Paris II University.

4 Words to remember (4 minutes)

Familiarize yourself with these words and then test yourself.

conference	**la conférence** *lah koñfayroñs*
trade fair	**la foire-exposition** *lah fwar-ekspohseesyoñ*
seminar	**le séminaire** *luh semeenair*
lecture theatre	**l'amphithéâtre** (m) *loñfeetayatruh*
conference room	**la salle de conférences** *lah sal duh koñfayroñs*
exhibition	**l'exposition** (f) *lekspohzeesyoñ*
library	**la bibliothèque** *lah biblee-yotek*
university lecturer	**le maître de conférences** *luh metruh duh koñfayroñs*
professor	**le professeur** *luh profesur*
medicine	**la médecine** *lah medseen*
science	**la science** *lah siyons*
literature	**la littérature** *lah leetairatyur*
engineering	**l'ingénierie** (f) *lahjayneeuree*

Nous avons un stand à la foire-exposition.
noo zavon uñ stond ah lah fwar ekspohseesyoñ
We have a stand at the trade fair.

5 Say it (2 minutes)

I'm doing research in medicine.

I have a degree in literature.

She's the professor.

Quel est votre secteur?
kel ay votruh sektur

What's your field?

Je fais de la recherche en ingénierie.
juh fay duh lah reshairsh oñ lahjayneeuree

I'm doing research in engineering.

Comme c'est intéressant.
kom say añtayraysoñ

How interesting.

1 **Warm up** (1 minute)

Ask "Can I ...?" (pp.34-5)

Say "I want to send an e-mail". (pp.80-1)

Ask "Can you send an e-mail?" (pp.80-1)

LES AFFAIRES
In business

You will receive a more friendly reception and make a good impression if you make the effort to begin a meeting with a short introduction in French, even if your vocabulary is limited. After that, all parties will probably be happy to continue the meeting in English.

2 **Words to remember** (6 minutes)

Familiarize yourself with these words and then test yourself by concealing the French with the cover flap.

le planning *luh planning*	schedule
la livraison *lah leevraysoñ*	delivery
le paiement *luh paymoñ*	payment
le budget *luh bujay*	budget
le prix *luh pree*	price
le document *luh dokoomoñ*	document
la facture *lah faktyur*	invoice
le devis *luh duhvees*	estimate
les bénéfices (m) *lay baynayfees*	profits
les ventes (f) *lay vont*	sales
les chiffres (m) *lay sheefruh*	figures

On signe le contrat?
oñ seenuh luh koñtrah
Shall we sign the contract?

le client
luh kleeyoñ
client

Cultural tip In general, commercial dealings are formal, but a lunch with wine is still part of doing business in France. As a client, you can expect to be taken out to a restaurant and as a supplier you should consider entertaining your customers.

3 Useful phrases (6 minutes)

Memorize these phrases. Note that when asking *what...?* you use **quel(s)** with masculine words but **quelle(s)** with feminine words.

le contrat
luh koñtrah
contract

le cadre
luh kadruh
executive

le rapport
luh rapor
report

Envoyez-moi le contrat s'il vous plaît.
oñvwayay mwah luh koñtrah, seel voo play

Please send me the contract.

Nous sommes convenus d'un planning?
noo som koñvunoo duñ planning

Have we agreed a schedule?

Quand pouvez-vous faire la livraison?
koñ poovay voo fair lah leevraysoñ

When can you make the delivery?

Quel est le budget?
kel ay luh bujay

What's the budget?

Vous pouvez m'envoyer la facture?
voo poovay moñvwayay lah faktyur

Can you send me the invoice?

4 Say it (2 minutes)

Can you send me the estimate?

Have we agreed a price?

What are the profits?

RÉVISEZ ET RÉPÉTEZ
Review and repeat

1 At the office

❶ **l'agraffeuse**
lagrafurz

❷ **la lampe**
lah lomp

❸ **l'ordinateur portable**
lordeenatur portabluh

❹ **le stylo**
luh steeloh

❺ **le bureau**
luh byuroh

❻ **le bloc-notes**
luh blok-not

❼ **la pendule**
lah poñdool

1 At the office (4 minutes)

Name these items.

lamp ❷ ❸ laptop

pen ❹

clock ❼

stapler ❶

❺ desk ❻ notepad

2 Jobs

❶ **médecin**
medsañ

❷ **plombier**
ploñbyay

❸ **commerçant**
comairsoñ(oñt)

❹ **comptable**
koñtabluh

❺ **professeur**
profesur

❻ **avocat**
avokah(aht)

2 Jobs (3 minutes)

What are these jobs in French?

❶ doctor

❷ plumber

❸ shopkeeper

❹ accountant

❺ teacher

❻ lawyer

3 Work (4 minutes)

Answer these questions following the English prompts.

Vous travaillez pour quelle compagnie?
❶ Say "I work for myself".

De quelle université êtes-vous?
❷ Say "I'm at the University of Bordeaux".

Quel est votre secteur?
❸ Say "I'm doing medical research".

Nous sommes convenus d'un planning?
❹ Say "Yes. Can you send me the budget?"

3 Work

❶ **Je suis à mon compte.**
juh swee zah moñ koñt

❷ **Je suis de l'université de Bordeaux.**
juh swee duh looneevair-sitay duh bordoe

❸ **Je fais de la recherche en médecine.**
juh fay duh lah reshairsh oñ medseen

❹ **Oui. Vous pouvez m'envoyer le budget?**
wee. voo poovay moñvwayay lah bujay

4 How much? (4 minutes)

Answer the question with the amount shown in brackets.

❶ **C'est combien le café?** (€2.50)

❷ **C'est combien la chambre?** (€47)

❸ **C'est combien pour un kilo de tomates?** (€3.25)

❹ **C'est combien l'emplacement pour quatre jours?** (€50)

4 How much?

❶ **C'est deux euros cinquante.**
say duh zuroh sankont

❷ **C'est quarante-sept euros.**
say sankont-set uroh

❸ **C'est trois euros vingt-cinq**
say twrah zuroh vañ-sank

❹ **C'est cinquante euros.**
say sankont uroh

1 Warm up (1 minute)

Say "I'm allergic to nuts". (pp.24-5)

Say the verb "avoir" (to have) in all its forms (je, tu, il/elle, vous, nous, ils/elles). (pp.14-5)

A LA PHARMACIE
At the chemist

French pharmacists study for seven years before qualifying. They can give advice about minor health problems and are permitted to dispense a wide variety of medicines, even giving injections, if necessary. There is a duty pharmacist (**pharmacie de garde**) in most towns.

2 Match and repeat (3 minutes)

Match the numbered items to the French words in the panel on the left and test yourself using the flap.

❶ **le bandage**
luh boñdarj

❷ **le sirop**
luh seeroe

❸ **les gouttes** (f)
lay goot

❹ **le pansement**
luh poñsumoñ

❺ **la seringue**
lah surañg

❻ **la crème**
lah krem

❼ **le suppositoire**
luh soopozitwar

❽ **le cachet**
luh kashay

syrup ❷

bandage ❶

❻ cream

drops ❸

plaster ❹

syringe ❺

3 In conversation (3 minutes)

Bonjour madame, vous désirez?
boñjoor, mad-dam. voo dayzeeray

Hello madam. What would you like?

J'ai mal à l'estomac.
jay mal ah lestomah

I have a stomach ache.

Vous avez la diarrhée?
voo zavay lah dyaray

Do you have diarrhoea?

4 Words to remember (2 minutes)

Familiarize yourself with these words and test yourself using the flap.

J'ai mal à la tête.
jay mal ah lah tet

I have a headache.

headache	**mal à la tête**
	mal ah lah tet
stomach ache	**mal à l'estomac**
	mal ah lestomah
diarrhoea	**la diarrhée**
	lah dyaray
cold	**un rhume**
	uñ room
cough	**une toux**
	oon too
sunburn	**un coup de soleil**
	uñ koo duh sol-lay
toothache	**mal aux dents**
	mal oh doñ

6 Say it (2 minutes)

I have a cold.

Do you have that as a cream?

Do you have a cough?

7 suppository

8 tablet

5 Useful phrases (4 minutes)

Familiarize yourself with these phrases and then test yourself using the cover flap.

I have sunburn.	**J'ai un coup de soleil.**
	jay uñ koo duh sol-lay
Do you have that as tablets?	**Vous avez des cachets à la place?**
	voo zavay day kashay ah lah plas
I'm allergic to penicillin.	**Je suis allergique à la pénicilline.**
	juh swee zalurgeek ah lah peneesilin

Non, mais j'ai aussi mal à la tête.
noñ, may jay osee mal ah lah tet

No, but I also have a headache.

Prenez ça.
prunay sah

Take this.

Vous avez un sirop à la place?
voo zavay uh seeroe ah lah plas

Do you have that as a syrup?

1 **Warm up** (1 minute)

Say " I have a toothache" and "I have sunburn". (pp.88-9)

Say the French for "red", "green", "black", and "yellow". (pp.74-5)

LE CORPS
The body

The most common phrase for talking about aches and pains is **J'ai mal à**... Don't forget that when **à** is placed in front of **le** it becomes **au** and in front of **les** it becomes **aux** (the **x** is silent). For example, **J'ai mal au dos** (*I have a backache*) and **J'ai mal aux oreilles** (*I have earache*).

2 **Match and repeat: body** (6 minutes)

Match the numbered parts of the body with the list on the left. Test yourself by using the cover flap.

❶ **la main**
lah mañ

❷ **la tête**
lah tet

❸ **l'épaule** (f)
laypoll

❹ **le coude**
luh kood

❺ **les cheveux**
lay shuhvuh

❻ **le bras**
luh brah

❼ **le cou**
luh koo

❽ **la poitrine**
lah pwatreen

❾ **l'estomac** (m)
lestomah

❿ **la jambe**
lah jomb

⓫ **le genou**
luh juhnoo

⓬ **le pied**
luh piyay

❶ hand
❹ elbow
❺ hair
❷ head
❻ arm
shoulder ❸
❼ neck
chest ❽
stomach ❾
leg ❿
knee ⓫
⓬ foot

3 Match and repeat: face (3 minutes)

Match the numbered facial features with the list on the right.

❶ le sourcil
luh soorsee

❷ l'œil (les yeux) (f)
luhyee (lay zyuh)

❸ le nez
luh nay

❹ la bouche
lah boosh

❺ l'oreille (f)
lor-ray

Labels on image: ❶ eyebrow, ❷ eye, ❺ ear, ❸ nose, ❹ mouth

4 Useful phrases (3 minutes)

Learn these phrases and then test yourself using the cover flap.

I have a pain in my back. **J'ai une douleur au dos.**
jay oon doolur oe doh

I have a rash on my arm. **J'ai une rougeur au bras.**
jay oon roojur oe brah

I don't feel well. **Je ne me sens pas bien.**
juh nuh muh soñ pah byañ

5 Put into practice (2 minutes)

Join in this conversation and test yourself using the cover flap.

Qu'est ce qui ne va pas? **Je ne me sens pas bien.**
keskee nuh vah pah *juh nuh muh soñ pah byañ*

What's the matter?

Say: I don't feel well.

Tu as mal où? **J'ai une douleur à l'épaule.**
tew ah mal oo *jay oon doolur ah laypoll*

Where does it hurt?

Say: I have a pain in my shoulder.

CHEZ LE DOCTEUR
At the doctor

Unless it's an emergency, you have to book an appointment with the doctor and pay when you leave. You can usually reclaim the money if you have medical insurance. You can find the names and addresses of local doctors from the local town hall or **syndicat d'initiative** (*tourist office*).

2 **Useful phrases you may hear** (3 minutes)

Familiarize yourself with these phrases and then test yourself using the cover flap to conceal the French on the left.

Ce n'est pas sérieux. *suh nay pah seryuh*	It's not serious.
Vous avez besoin de tests. *voo zavay buzwañ duh test*	You need to have tests.
Vous avez une infection aux reins. *voo zavay oon añfeksyoñ oh rañ*	You have a kidney infection.
Vous avez besoin d'aller à l'hôpital. *voo zavay buzwañ dalay ah lopeetal*	You need to go to hospital.

Vous prenez des médicaments?
voo prunay day maydikamoñ
Are you taking any medications?

3 **In conversation** (5 minutes)

Qu'est-ce qui ne va pas?
keskee nuh vah pah

What's the matter?

J'ai une douleur à la poitrine.
jay oon doolur ah lah pwatreen

I have a pain in my chest.

Laissez-moi vous examiner.
lessay-mwah voo zekzaminay

Let me examine you.

4 Useful phrases you may need to say (4 minutes)

Je suis enceinte.
juh swee zoñsant
I'm pregnant.

Practise these phrases and then test yourself using the cover flap.

I'm diabetic.	**Je suis diabétique.** *juh swee diyabeteek*
I'm epileptic.	**Je suis épileptique.** *juh swee zepeelepteek*
I'm asthmatic.	**Je suis asthmatique.** *juh swee zasmateek*
I have a heart condition.	**J'ai un problème au cœur.** *jay uñ prob-lem* *oh kur*
I feel faint.	**Je vais m'évanouir.** *juh vay mayvanooweer*
I have a fever.	**J'ai de la fièvre.** *jay duh lah fyevruh*
It's urgent.	**C'est urgent.** *say turjoñ*

Cultural tip
If you are an EU national, you are entitled to free emergency medical treatment in France on production of a European Health Insurance Card or E111 form. For an ambulance call 112.

5 Say it (2 minutes)

Do I need tests?

My son needs to go to hospital.

It's not urgent.

C'est sérieux?
say seryuh

Is it serious?

Non, vous avez seulement une indigestion.
noñ, voo zavay surlmoñ oon añdeejestyoñ

No, you only have indigestion.

Quel soulagement!
kel soolarjemoñ

What a relief!

1 **Warm up** (1 minute)

Ask "How long is the journey?" (pp.42-3)

How do you ask "Do I need...?" (pp.92-3)

What is the French for "mouth" and "head"? (pp.90-1)

A L'HÔPITAL
At the hospital

The main hospitals in France are attached to universities and are known as **Centres Hospitaliers Universitaires** (CHU). It is useful to know a few basic phrases relating to hospitals for use in an emergency or in case you need to visit a friend or colleague in hospital.

2 **Useful phrases** (5 minutes)

Familiarize yourself with these phrases. Conceal the French with the cover flap and test yourself.

Quelles sont les heures de visite? *kel soñ lay zur duh vizeet*	What are the visiting hours?
Ça va prendre combien de temps? *sah vah prondruh koñbyañ duh toñ*	How long will it take?
Ça va faire mal? *sah vah fair mal*	Will it hurt?
Allongez-vous ici, s'il vous plaît. *aloñjay voo zeesee, seel voo play*	Please lie down here.
Vous ne devez pas manger. *voo nuh duvay pah moñjay*	You must not eat.
Ne bougez pas la tête. *nuh boojay pah lah tet*	Don't move your head.
Ouvrez la bouche, s'il vous plaît. *oovray lah boosh, seel voo play*	Please open your mouth.
Vous avez besoin d'une prise de sang. *voo zavay buzwañ doon preez duh soñ*	You need a blood test.

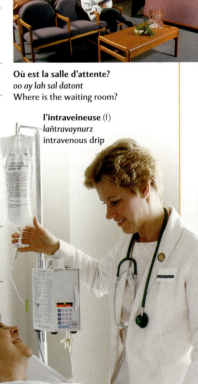

Où est la salle d'attente?
oo ay lah sal datont
Where is the waiting room?

l'intraveineuse (f)
lañtravaynurz
intravenous drip

Ça va mieux?
sah vah meeyuh
Are you feeling better?

3 Words to remember (4 minutes)

Memorize these words and test yourself using the cover flap.

emergency department	**la salle des urgences** *lah sal day zurjoñs*
children's ward	**le service de pédiatrie** *luh survees duh paydyah-tree*
operating theatre	**la salle d'opération** *lah sal dopairasyoñ*
x-ray department	**la salle de radiologie** *lah sal duh radyo-lojee*
waiting room	**la salle d'attente** *lah sal datont*
lift	**l'ascenseur** *lasoñsur*
stairs	**les escaliers** *lay zeskalyay*

Votre radio est normale.
votruh radyoh ay normal
Your x-ray is normal.

4 Put into practice (3 minutes)

Join in this conversation. Read the French on the left and follow the instructions to make your reply. Then test yourself by concealing the answers with the cover flap.

Vous avez une infection.
voo zavay oon añfeksyoñ

You have an infection.

Ask: Do I need tests?

J'ai besoin de tests?
jay buzwañ duh test

Tout d'abord, vous avez besoin d'une prise de sang.
too dabor, voo zavay buzwañ doon preez duh soñ

First you will need a blood test.

Ask: Will it hurt?

Ça va faire mal?
sah vah fair mal

5 Say it (2 minutes)

Does he need a blood test?

Where is the children's ward?

Do I need an x-ray?

Non, ne vous inquiétez pas.
noñ, nuh voo zañkyatay pah

No. Don't worry.

Ask: How long will it take?

Ça va prendre combien de temps?
sah vah prondruh koñbyañ duh toñ

Réponses
Answers (Cover with flap)

RÉVISEZ ET RÉPÉTEZ
Review and repeat

1 The body

1 la tête
lah tet

2 le bras
luh brah

3 la poitrine
lah pwatreen

4 l'estomac
lestomah

5 la jambe
lah jomb

6 le genou
luh juhnoo

7 le pied
luh piyay

1 The body (4 minutes)

Name the numbered
body parts in French.

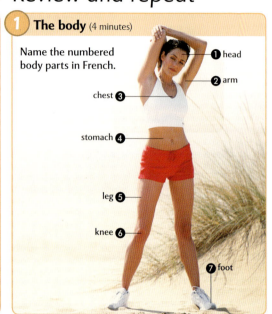

- **1** head
- **2** arm
- chest **3**
- stomach **4**
- leg **5**
- knee **6**
- **7** foot

2 On the phone

1 Je voudrais parler à
Caroline Martin.
*juh voodray parlay ah
karoleen martañ*

2 [your name] de
l'imprimerie
Laporte.
*[your name] duh
lahpreemuree laport*

3 Je peux laisser
un message?
*juh puh laysay
uñ mesarj*

4 C'est bon pour le
rendez-vous lundi à
onze heures.
*say boñ poor luh
roñday-voo lañdee
ah onz ur*

5 Merci, au revoir.
mairsee, ovwar

2 On the phone (4 minutes)

You are arranging an appointment. Follow the
conversation, replying in French following
the English prompts.

Allô, société Apex.
1 I'd like to speak to
Caroline Martin.

**Oui, c'est de la part
de qui?**
2 [your name] of Laporte
printers.

**Je suis désolé, la ligne
est occupée.**
3 Can I leave a message?

Oui, bien sûr.
4 It's fine for the
appointment on
Monday at 11am.

Très bien, au revoir.
5 Thank you, goodbye.

Réponses
Answers (Cover with flap)

3 Clothing (3 minutes)

Say the French words for the numbered items of clothing.

tie ❶

❷ jacket

❹ skirt

trousers ❸

❻ tights

shoes ❺

3 Clothing

❶ **la cravate**
lah kravat

❷ **la veste**
lah vest

❸ **le pantalon**
luh poñtaloñ

❹ **la jupe**
lah joop

❺ **les chaussures**
lay shohsyur

❻ **les collants**
lay kolloñ

4 At the doctor's (4 minutes)

Say these phrases in French.

❶ I don't feel well.
❷ Do I need tests?
❸ I have a heart condition.
❹ Do I need to go to hospital?
❺ I am pregnant.

4 At the doctor's

❶ **Je ne me sens pas bien.**
juh nuh muh soñ pah byañ

❷ **J'ai besoin de tests.**
jay buzwañ duh test

❸ **J'ai un problème au cœur.**
jay uñ prob-lem oh kur

❹ **J'ai besoin d'aller à l'hôpital.**
jay buzwañ dallay ah lopeetal

❺ **Je suis enceinte.**
juh swee zoñsant

CHEZ NOUS
At home

1 **Warm up** (1 minute)

Say the months of the year in French. (pp.28-9)

Ask "Is there an art gallery?" (pp.48-9) and "How many brothers do you have?" (pp.14-5)

Many city-dwellers live in an apartment block (**l'immeuble**), but in rural areas the houses tend to be detached (**individuelle**). If you want to know the total number of rooms you will need to ask "**Combien de pièces?**". If you want to know how many bedrooms, ask "**Combien de chambres?**"

2 **Match and repeat** (5 minutes)

Match the numbered items to the list and test yourself using the flap.

❶ **la fenêtre**
   lah fenaytruh

❷ **la cheminée**
   lah shemnay

❸ **le toit**
   lah twut

❹ **la gouttière**
   lah gootyair

❺ **le mur**
   luh myur

❻ **le volet**
   luh volay

❼ **la porte**
   lah port

❽ **le passage**
   luh passarj

chimney ❷

window ❶

❺ wall

❻ shutter

Cultural tip Most French houses have shutters (**volets**) at each window. These are closed at night and in the heat of the day. Curtains, where they are present, tend to be more for decoration. A single-storey bungalow is known as **un pavillon** and these are popular among the French as holiday homes in tourist resorts.

3 Words to remember (4 minutes)

Quel est le loyer par mois?
kel ay luh lwayay par mwah?
What is the rent per month?

Familiarize yourself with these words and test yourself using the flap.

room	**la pièce**	*lah piyes*
floor	**le sol**	*luh sol*
ceiling	**le plafond**	*luh plafoñ*
bedroom	**la chambre**	*lah shombruh*
bathroom	**la salle de bains**	*lah sal duh bañ*
kitchen	**la cuisine**	*lah kwiseen*
dining room	**la salle à manger**	*lah sal ah moñjay*
living room	**le salon**	*luh saloñ*
cellar	**la cave**	*lah kav*
attic	**le grenier**	*luh grunyay*

❸ roof

❹ gutter

4 Useful phrases (3 minutes)

Learn these phrases and test yourself.

Il y a un garage?
eelyah uh gararj

Is there a garage?

C'est disponible quand?
say deesponeebluh koñ

When is it available?

C'est meublé?
say murblay

Is it furnished?

❽ driveway   door ❼

5 Say it (2 minutes)

Is there a dining room?

Is it large?

Is it available in July?

1 Warm up (1 minute)

What is the French for "room" (pp.58–9), "desk" (pp.80–1), "bed" (pp.60–1), and "toilet(s)"? (pp.52–3)

How do you say "soft", "beautiful", and "big"? (pp.64–5)

DANS LA MAISON
In the house

When you rent a house or villa in France, it is usual to be asked to pay for services such as electricity and gas in addition to the basic weekly or monthly rent. Additional charges might also extend to wood or other fuel for an open fire, which is usually charged by the cubic metre.

2 Match and repeat (3 minutes)

Match the numbered items to the list in the panel on the left. Then test yourself by concealing the French with the cover flap.

❶ **le plan de travail**
  luh plañ duh traveye

❷ **l'évier** (m)
  levyay

❸ **le micro-ondes**
  luh meekro-ond

❹ **la cuisinière**
  lah kwiseenyair

❺ **le four**
  luh foor

❻ **le frigo**
  luh freegoh

❼ **la table**
  lah tabluh

❽ **la chaise**
  lah shez

❹ cooker ❶ worktop ❻ fridge

chair ❽ table ❼ ❺ oven

3 In conversation (3 minutes)

C'est le four.
say luh foor

This is the oven.

Il y a un lave-vaisselle aussi?
eelyah uñ lav-vaysel osee

Is there a dishwasher as well?

Oui, et il y a un grand congélateur.
wee, ay eelyah uñ groñ koñjelatur

Yes, and there's a big freezer.

4 Words to remember (2 minutes)

Familiarize yourself with these words and test yourself using the flap.

wardrobe	**l'armoire** (f) *larmwar*
armchair	**le fauteuil** *luh fohtuhee*
chest of drawers	**la commode** *lah komohd*
fireplace	**la cheminée** *lah shemnay*
carpet	**le tapis** *luh tapee*
bathtub	**la baignoire** *lah bainwar*
wash basin	**le lavabo** *luh lavabo*
curtains	**les rideaux** (m) *lay ridoe*

Le canapé est neuf.
luh kanapay ay nurf
The sofa is new.

❷ sink   microwave ❸

5 Useful phrases (4 minutes)

Practise these phrases and then test yourself using the cover flap to conceal the French.

Is electricity included?	**L'électricité est inclue?** *laylektreesitay et añkloo*
I don't like the curtains.	**Je n'aime pas les rideaux.** *juh nem pah lay ridoe*
The carpet is old.	**Le tapis est vieux.** *luh tapee ay vyuh*

6 Say it (2 minutes)

Is there a microwave?

I like the fireplace.

What a soft sofa!

L'évier est neuf?
levyay ay nurf

Is the sink new?

Bien sûr. Et voilà la machine à laver.
byañ syur. ay vwalah lah masheen ah lavay

Of course. And here's the washing machine.

Quel beau carrelage!
kel boe karlarj

What beautiful tiles!

LE JARDIN
The garden

Say "I need", "you need", "he needs". (pp.64-5, pp.92-4)

What is the French for "day", "week", and "month"? (pp.28-9)

Say the days of the week. (pp.28-9)

The garden of a house or villa may be communal, or at least partly shared. Check with the estate agent. In general, French gardens are well-kept and reasonably formal. The natural, "wild" look is not very popular and hedges are usually carefully trimmed and lawns are regularly mown.

2 **Words to remember** (3 minutes)

Familiarize yourself with these words and test yourself using the flap.

la tondeuse à gazon *lah toñdurz ah gazoñ*	lawn mower
la fourche *lah foorsh*	fork
la bêche *lah besh*	spade
le râteau *luh ratoe*	rake
la jardinerie *lah jardañree*	garden centre

terrace ❶

tree ❷

flowers ❼

❽ weeds

soil ❸   path ❾

3 **Useful phrases** (4 minutes)

Familarize yourself with these phrases and then test yourself.

The gardener comes once a week.	**Le jardinier vient une fois par semaine.** *luh jardañyay vyañ oon fwah par suhmayn*
Can you mow the lawn?	**Vous pouvez tondre la pelouse?** *voo poovay toñdruh lah pelooz*
Is the garden private?	**Le jardin est privé?** *luh jardañ ay preevay*
The garden needs watering.	**Le jardin a besoin d'eau.** *luh jardañ ah buzwañ doe*

❺ hedge

❹ lawn

❻ plants

❿ flowerbed

4 **Match and repeat** (5 minutes)

Match the numbered items to the words in the panel on the right.

❶ **la terrasse**
lah terass

❷ **l'arbre** (m)
larbruh

❸ **la terre**
lah tair

❹ **la pelouse**
lah pelooz

❺ **la haie**
lah ay

❻ **les plantes** (f)
lay ploñt

❼ **les fleurs** (f)
lay flur

❽ **les mauvaises herbes** (f)
lay movay zurb

❾ **l'allée** (f)
lallay

❿ **le parterre de fleurs**
luh partair duh flur

5 **Say it** (2 minutes)

The lawn needs watering.

Are there any trees?

The gardener comes on Fridays.

Say "My name's John".
(pp.8-9)

How do you say "Don't
worry"? (pp.94-5)

What's "your" in French?
(pp.12-3)

LES ANIMAUX
Pets

"Pet passports" are now available to enable
holiday-makers and commuters to take their
pets with them to France and avoid quarantine
on return to the United Kingdom. Consult your
vet for details of how to obtain the necessary
vaccinations and paperwork.

2 **Match and repeat** (3 minutes)

Match the numbered animals to the French
words in the panel on the left. Then test
yourself using the cover flap.

❶ **le chat**
luh shah

❷ **le lapin**
luh lapañ

❸ **l'oiseau** (m)
lwazoe

❹ **le poisson**
luh pwassoñ

❺ **le chien**
luh shiañ

❻ **le hamster**
luh amstair

bird ❸

❷ rabbit

dog ❺

❶ cat

3 **Useful phrases** (4 minutes)

Familiarize yourself with these phrases and
then test yourself using the cover flap.

Ce chien est gentil? *suh shiañ ay joñtee*	Is this dog friendly?
Je peux amener mon chien? *juh puh amunay moñ shiañ*	Can I bring my dog?
J'ai peur des chats. *jay pur day shah*	I'm frightened of cats.
Mon chien ne mord pas. *moñ shiañ nuh mor pah*	My dog doesn't bite.

Ce chat est plein de puces.
suh shah ay plañ duh pous
This cat is full of fleas.

Cultural tip Many dogs in France are guard dogs and you may encounter them tethered or roaming free. Approach farms and rural houses with care, and keep away from the dog's territory. Look out for warning notices such as **Attention au chien** (*Beware of the dog*).

ATTENTION AU CHIEN

4 **Words to remember** (4 minutes)

Memorize these words and test yourself using the cover flap.

vet	**le vétérinaire** *luh vetairinair*
vaccination	**la vaccination** *lah vaksinasyoñ*
pet passport	**le passeport d'animaux** *luh passpor danimoe*
basket	**le panier** *luh panyay*
cage	**la cage** *lah karj*
bowl	**la gamelle** *lah gamel*
collar	**le collier** *luh kolyay*
lead	**la laisse** *lah less*
fleas	**les puces** (f) *lay pous*

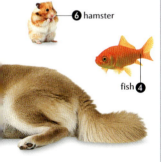

Mon chien est malade.
moñ shiañ ay malahd
My dog is not well.

6 hamster

fish **4**

5 **Put into practice** (3 minutes)

Join in this conversation. Read the French on the left and follow the instructions to make your reply. Then test yourself by concealing the answers with the cover flap.

C'est votre chien?
say votruh shiañ

Oui, il s'appelle Sandy.
wee, eel sapell Sandy

Is this your dog?

Say: Yes, he's called Sandy.

J'ai peur des chiens.
jay pur day shiañ

Ne vous inquiétez pas. Il est gentil.
nuh voo zañkyatay pah. eel ay joñtee

I'm frightened of dogs.

Say: Don't worry. He's friendly.

RÉVISEZ ET RÉPÉTEZ
Review and repeat

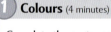

1 Colours

❶ **noir**
nwar

❷ **blanche**
blonsh

❸ **rouge**
rooj

❹ **verte**
vairt

❺ **jaunes**
jon

1 Colours (4 minutes)

Complete the sentences with the French for the colour in brackets. Be careful to choose the correct masculine or feminine form.

❶ **Vous avez cette veste en _____ ? (black)**

❷ **Je prends la jupe _____. (white)**

❸ **Vous avez cette robe en _____? (red)**

❹ **Non mais j'ai une _____. (green)**

❺ **Vous avez des chaussettes _____?
(yellow)**

2 Kitchen

❶ **la cuisinière**
lah kwiseenyair

❷ **le frigo**
luh freegoh

❸ **l'évier**
levyay

❹ **le micro-ondes**
luh meekro-ond

❺ **le four**
luh foor

❻ **la chaise**
lah shez

❼ **la table**
lah tabluh

2 Kitchen (4 minutes)

Say the French words for the numbered items.

cooker ❶   fridge ❷

❺ oven   chair ❻

3 House (4 minutes)

You are visiting a house in France. Join in the conversation, replying in French following the English prompts.

Voilà le salon.
❶ What a lovely fireplace!

Oui, et il y a aussi une grande cuisine.
❷ How many bedrooms?

Il y a trois chambres.
❸ Do you have a garage?

Non, mais il y a un grand jardin.
❹ When is it available?

Juillet.
❺ What is the rent a month?

3 House

❶ **Quelle belle cheminée!**
kel bel shemnay

❷ **Combien de chambres?**
koñbyañ duh shombruh

❸ **Vous avez un garage?**
voo zavay uñ gararj

❹ **C'est disponible quand?**
say deesponeebluh koñ

❺ **Quel est le loyer par mois?**
kel ay luh lwayay par mwah

microwave ❹

❸ sink

table ❼

4 At home (3 minutes)

Say the French for the following items:

❶ washing machine
❷ sofa
❸ attic
❹ dining room
❺ tree
❻ garden

4 At home

❶ **la machine à laver**
lah masheen ah lavay

❷ **le canapé**
luh kanapay

❸ **le grenier**
luh grunyay

❹ **la salle à manger**
lah sal ah moñjay

❺ **l'arbre**
larbruh

❻ **le jardin**
luh jardañ

LA POSTE ET LA BANQUE
Post and bank

1 Warm up (1 minute)

Ask "How do I get to the bank?" and "How do I get to the post office?" (pp.68–9)

What's the French for "passport"? (pp.54–5)

Ask "What time?" (pp.30–1)

The post office also serves as a bank. You do not need to queue at the cashier, as there are normally cashpoints available outside the building. Stamps are also available from **le tabac** (*bar/tobacconists*).

2 Words to remember: post (3 minutes)

la boîte postale *lah bwat post-tal*	post box
la carte postale *lah kart post-tal*	postcard
le colis *luh kolee*	parcel
par avion *par avyoñ*	air mail
en recommandé *oñ rukomoñday*	registered post
le timbre *luh tambruh*	stamp
le code postal *luh kod post-tal*	postcode
le facteur *luh faktur*	postman

Familiarize yourself with these words and test yourself using the cover flap to conceal the French on the left.

C'est combien pour le Royaume-Uni?
say koñbyañ poor luh royom oonee
How much is it for the United Kingdom?

l'enveloppe (f)
loñvuhlop
envelope

3 In conversation (3 minutes)

Je voudrais retirer de l'argent.
juh voodray ruteeray duh larjoñ

I'd like to withdraw some money.

Vous avez une identification?
voo zavay oon eedoñtee-fikasyoñ

Do you have any identification?

Oui, voilà mon passeport.
wee, vwalah moñ passpor

Yes, here's my passport.

4 Words to remember: bank (2 minutes)

Familiarize yourself with these words and test yourself using the cover flap to conceal the French on the right.

la carte bancaire
lah kart boñkair
bank card

Comment je peux payer?
komon juh puh payay
How can I pay?

PIN	**le code** *luh kod*
bank	**la banque** *lah boñk*
cashier	**le guichet** *luh geeshay*
notes	**les billets** *lay beeyay*
ATM/cashpoint	**le distributeur automatique** *luh distreebootur otomateek*
credit card	**la carte de crédit** *lah kart duh kraydee*

5 Useful phrases (4 minutes)

Learn these phrases and then test yourself using the cover flap.

I'd like to change some money.	**Je voudrais changer de l'argent.** *juh voodray shoñjay duh larjoñ*
What is the exchange rate?	**Quel est le taux de change?** *kel ay luh toe duh shoñj*
I'd like to withdraw some money.	**Je voudrais retirer de l'argent.** *juh voodray ruteeray duh larjoñ*

6 Say it (2 minutes)

I'd like a stamp for the United Kingdom.

Can I pay by credit card?

Do I need my PIN?

Composez votre code s'il vous plaît.
komposay votruh kod seel voo play

Please key in your PIN.

J'ai besoin de signer aussi?
jay buzwañ duh seenyay ohsee

Do I need to sign as well?

Non, ce n'est pas nécessaire.
noñ, suh nay pah nesesair

No, that's not necessary.

LES SERVICES
Services

You can combine the French words on these pages with the vocabulary you learned in week 10 to help you explain basic problems and cope with arranging most repairs. When organizing building work or a repair, it's a good idea to agree the price and method of payment in advance.

2 **Words to remember** (4 minutes)

Familiarize yourself with these words and test yourself using the flap.

le plombier *luh ploñbyay*	plumber
l'électricien (m) *laylektreesyañ*	electrician
le garagiste *luh gararjeest*	mechanic
le constructeur *luh koñstruktur*	builder
la femme de ménage *lah fam duh maynarj*	cleaner
le décorateur *luh daykoratur*	decorator
le charpentier *luh sharpañtyay*	carpenter
le maçon *luh massoñ*	bricklayer

la manivelle
lah maneevel
wrench

Je n'ai pas besoin d'un garagiste.
juh nay pah buzwañ duñ gararjeest
I don't need a mechanic.

3 **In conversation** (3 minutes)

La machine à laver est en panne.
lah masheen ah lavay ay toñ pan

The washing machine has broken down.

Oui, le tuyeau est cassé.
wee luh tweeyoh ay kassay

Yes, the hose is broken.

Vous pouvez la réparer?
voo poovay lah rayparay

Can you repair it?

4 **Useful phrases** (3 minutes)

Learn these phrases and then test yourself using the cover flap.

Please clean the bathroom.	**Nettoyez la salle de bain, s'il vous plait.** *netwuhyay lah sal duh bañ seel voo play*
Can you repair the boiler?	**Vous pouvez réparer la chaudière?** *voo poovay rayparay lah shodyair*
Do you know a good electrician?	**Vous connaissez un bon électricien?** *voo konessay uñ boñ aylektreesyañ*

Je peux faire réparer ça où?
juh puh fair rayparay sah oo
Where can I get this repaired?

5 **Put into practice** (4 minutes)

Practise these phrases. Cover up the text on the right and complete the dialogue in French. Check your answers and repeat if necessary.

Votre clôture est cassée.
votruh klotoor ay kassay

Your fence is broken.

Ask: Do you know a good builder?

Vous connaissez un bon constructeur?
voo konessay uh boñ koñstruktur

Oui, il y en a un dans le village.
wee, eelyonah uñ doñ luh villarj

Yes, there is one in the village.

Ask: Do you have his phone number?

Vous avez son numéro de téléphone?
voo zavay soñ noomairoe duh telayfon

Non, vous avez besoin d'un nouveau.
noñ. voo zavay buzwañ duñ noovoh

No, you need a new one.

Vous pouvez faire ça aujourd'hui?
voo poovay fair sah oh-joordwee

Can you do it today?

Non, je reviens demain.
non, juh ruvyañ dumañ

No. I'll come back tomorrow.

VENIR
To come

Say the days of the week in French. (pp.28–9)

How do you say "cleaner"? (pp.110–11)

Say "It's 9.30", "10.45", and "12.00". (pp.10-11, pp.30-1)

The verb **venir** (to come) is another important verb. Other useful verbs are made up of **venir** with a prefix, such as **revenir** (to come back) and **devenir** (to become). These can be formed in the same way as **venir** (below). Remember that **je viens** can mean either I come or I am coming.

2 Venir: to come (6 minutes)

Say the different forms of **venir** (to come) aloud. Use the cover flap to test yourself and, when you are confident, practise the sample sentences below.

je viens *juh vyañ*	I come
tu viens *tew vyañ*	you come (informal singular)
il/elle vient *eel/el vyañ*	he/she comes
nous venons *noo vunoñ*	we come
vous venez *voo vunay*	you come (formal singular or plural)
ils/elles viennent *eel/el vyen*	they come
Je viens de New York. *juh vyañ duh noo york*	I come from New York.
Nous venons tous les mardis. *noo vunoñ too lay mardee*	We come every Tuesday.
Ils viennent par le train. *eel vyen par luh trañ*	They come by train.

Il vient de Chine.
eel vyañ duh sheen
He comes from China.

Conversational tip You can use the phrase **je viens de...** (literally *I come from...*) to talk about something you have just done or have recently completed. For example **je viens de faire les courses** (*I have just done the shopping*) or **je viens d'envoyer un email** (*I have just sent an e-mail*). To say *just* in the sense of *only*, as in *I eat just a sandwich for lunch*, the French use **seulement**: **je mange seulement un sandwich pour déjeuner**.

3 Useful phrases (4 minutes)

Learn these phrases and then test yourself using the cover flap.

When can I come?	**Je peux venir quand?** *juh puh vuneer koñ*
Where does she come from?	**Elle vient d'où?** *el vyañ doo*
The cleaner comes every Monday.	**La femme de ménage vient tous les lundis.** *lah fam duh maynarj vyañ too lay luñdee*
Come with me. (informal/formal)	**Viens avec moi./ Venez avec moi.** *vyañ avek mwah/ vunay avek mwah*

Je viens de me réveiller.
juh vyañ duh muh rayvay-yay
I have just woken up.

4 Put into practice (4 minutes)

Join in this conversation. Read the French on the left and follow the instructions to make your reply. Then test yourself by concealing the answers with the cover flap.

Bonjour, salon de coiffure Christine.
boñjoor, saloñ duh kwafur Christine

Hello, this is Christine's hair salon.

Say: I'd like an appointment.

Je voudrais un rendez-vous.
juh voodray uñ roñday-voo

Vous voulez venir quand?
voo voolay vuneer koñ

When do you want to come?

Say: Can I come today?

Je peux venir aujourd'hui?
juh puh vuneer oh-joordwee

Oui bien sûr, à quelle heure?
wee byañ syur, ah kel ur

Yes of course, what time?

Say: At 10.30.

A dix heures et demie.
ah deez ur ay dumee

LA POLICE ET LE CRIME
Police and crime

1 **Warm up** (1 minute)

What's the French for "big/tall" and "small/short"? (pp.64-5)

Say "The room is big" and "The bed is small". (pp.64-5)

If you are the victim of a crime while in France, you should go to a police station to report it. In an emergency you can dial 112. You may have to explain your complaint in French, so some basic vocabulary is useful. In the event of a burglary, the police will usually come to the house.

2 **Words to remember: crime** (4 minutes)

Familiarize yourself with these words.

J'ai besoin d'un avocat.
jay buzwañ duñ avokah
I need a lawyer.

le cambriolage *luh kañbryolarj*	burglary
le rapport de police *luh rapor duh polees*	police report
le voleur *luh volur*	thief
la police *lah polees*	police
la déposition *lah daypoziyoñ*	statement
le témoin *luh taymwañ*	witness
l'avocat(e) *lavokah(aht)*	lawyer

3 **Useful phrases** (3 minutes)

Memorize these phrases and then test yourself using the cover flap.

J'ai été cambriolé(e). *jay aytay kañbryolay*	I've been burgled.
Qu'est-ce qui a été volé? *keskee ah aytay volay*	What was stolen?
Vous avez vu qui a fait ça? *voo zavay voo kee ah fay sah*	Did you see who did it?
Ça s'est passé quand? *sah say passay koñ*	When did it happen?

l'appareil-photo
lapareye foto
camera

le porte-monnaie
luh port mohnay
purse

4 Words to remember: appearance (5 minutes)

Learn these words. Remember some adjectives have a feminine form.

Il est chauve avec une barbe.
eel ay shohv avek oon barb
He is bald and has a beard.

Il a les cheveux noirs et courts.
eel ah lay shuvuh nwar ay kor
He has short, black hair.

man	**l'homme** (m) *lom*
woman	**la femme** *lah fam*
tall	**grand/grande** *groñ/groñd*
short	**petit/petite** *puhtee/puhteet*
young	**jeune** *juhn*
old	**vieux/vieille** *vyuh/vyay*
fat	**gros/grosse** *groe/gros*
thin	**maigre** *maygruh*
long/short hair	**les cheveux longs/ courts** (m) *lay shuvuh loñ/kor*
spectacles	**les lunettes** (f) *lay loonet*
beard	**la barbe** *lah barb*

Cultural tip In France there is a difference between **la gendarmerie** and **la police**. **La gendarmerie** operates in smaller towns and **la police** in major cities. Their appearance and uniform are similar and officers from both forces carry guns.

5 Put into practice (2 minutes)

Practise these phrases. Then cover up the text on the right and follow the instructions to make your reply in French.

Il ressemblait à quoi?   **Petit et gros.**
eel ruzoñblay ah kwah   *puhtee ay groe*

What did he look like?

Say: Short and fat.

Et les cheveux?   **Longs avec une barbe.**
ay lay shuvuh   *loñ avek oon barb*

And the hair?

Say: Long with a beard.

Réponses
Answers (Cover with flap)

RÉVISEZ ET RÉPÉTEZ
Review and repeat

1 To come

❶ **viviens**
vyañ

❷ **vient**
vyañ

❸ **venons**
vunoñ

❹ **venez**
vunay

❺ **viennent**
vyen

1 To come (3 minutes)

Put the correct form of **venir** (*to come*) into the gaps.

❶ Je _____ à quatre heures.

❷ Le jardinier _____ une fois par semaine.

❸ Nous _____ pour déjeuner mardi.

❹ Vous _____ avec nous?

❺ Mes parents _____ par le train.

2 Bank and post

❶ **le colis**
luh kolee

❷ **les timbres**
lay tambruh

❸ **les cartes postales**
lay kart post-tal

❹ **les billets**
lay biyay

❺ **la carte bancaire**
lah kart boñkair

2 Bank and post (4 minutes)

Say the French words for the following numbered items:

stamps ❷

❶ parcel

❸ postcards

❹ notes

bank card ❺

Réponses
Answers (Cover with flap)

3 Appearance (4 minutes)

What do these descriptions mean?

1 C'est un homme grand et maigre.

2 Elle a les cheveux courts et des lunettes.

3 Je suis petite et j'ai les cheveux longs.

4 Elle est vieille et grosse.

5 Il a les yeux bleus et une barbe.

3 Appearance

1 He's a tall thin man.

2 She has short hair and glasses.

3 I'm short and I have long hair.

4 She is old and fat.

5 He has blue eyes and a beard.

4 The pharmacy (4 minutes)

You are asking a pharmacist for advice. Join in the conversation, replying in French following the English prompts.

> Bonjour. Je peux vous aider?

1 I have a cough.

> Et vous avez aussi un rhume?

2 No, but I have a headache.

> Prenez ces cachets.

3 Do you have that as a syrup?

> Bien sûr. Voilà.

4 Thank you. How much is that?

> Six euros.

5 Here you are. Goodbye.

4 The pharmacy

1 J'ai une toux.
jay oon too

2 Non, mai j'ai mal à la tête.
noñ. may jay mal ah lah tet

3 Vous avez un sirop à la place?
voo zavay uñ seeroe ah lah plas

4 Merci. C'est combien?
mairsee. say koñbyañ

5 Voilà. Au revoir.
vwalah. ovwar

LES LOISIRS
Leisure time

The French pride themselves on their support for the arts, including opera and film. It would not be unusual to number politics or philosophy among your interests. Phrasebooks aimed at French speakers often have a section on useful conversational openers for these topics.

① Warm up (1 minute)

What is the French for "museum" and "art gallery"? (pp.48-9)

Say "I don't like the curtains". (pp.100-1)

Ask "Do you want...?" informally (pp.22-3)

② Words to remember (4 minutes)

J'adore l'opéra.
jador lopayra
I love opera.

Familiarize yourself with these words and test yourself using the cover flap to conceal the French on the left.

le théâtre *luh tay-atruh*	theatre
le cinéma *luh sinaymah*	cinema
la discothèque *lah diskotek*	disco
la musique *lah moozeek*	music
l'art (m) *lar*	art
le sport *luh spor*	sport
le tourisme *luh torizmuh*	sightseeing
les jeux vidéos *lay juh viday-oh*	computer games

③ In conversation (4 minutes)

Salut, tu veux jouer au tennis aujourd'hui?
saloo, tew vuh jooay oh tenees oh-joordwee

Hi, do you want to play tennis today?

Non. Je n'aime pas le sport.
noñ. juh nem pah luh spor

No, I don't like sport.

Alors, quels sont tes intérêts?
alor, kel soñ tay zañtairay

So what are your interests?

Je déteste la guitare.
juh daytest lah geetar
I hate guitar music.

4 Useful phrases (4 minutes)

Learn these phrases and then test yourself using the cover flap.

What are your (formal/ informal) interests?	**Quels sont vos/tes intérêts?** *kel soñ voe/tay zañtayray*
I like the theatre.	**J'aime le théâtre.** *jem luh tay-atruh*
I prefer the cinema.	**Je préfère le cinéma.** *juh prayfair luh sinaymah*
I'm interested in art.	**Je m'intéresse à l'art.** *juh mañtairess ah lar*
That bores me.	**Ça m'ennuie.** *sah moñwee*

les spectateurs (m)
lay spektahtur
audience

la galerie
lah galuree
circle

l'orchestre (m)
lorkestruh
stalls

5 Say it (2 minutes)

I'm interested in music.

I prefer sport.

I don't like computer games.

Je préfère le shopping.
juh prayfair luh shopping

I prefer shopping.

Ça ne m'intéresse pas.
sah nuh mañtairess pah

That doesn't interest me.

Pas de problème. J'y vais toute seule.
pah de prob-lem. jee vay toot surl

No problem. I'll go on my own.

LE SPORT ET LES PASSE-TEMPS
Sport and hobbies

1 **Warm up** (1 minute)

Ask "Do you (formal) want to play tennis?" (pp.118-19)

Say "I like the theatre" and "I prefer sightseeing". (pp.118-19)

Say "That doesn't interest me". (pp.118-19)

The verb **faire** (*to do or to make*) is a useful verb for talking about hobbies. **Faire** is followed by **du, de la** or **de l'**: **Je fais de la peinture** (*I paint*). You can also use the verb **jouer** (*to play*) when talking about playing sports and music.

2 **Words to remember** (5 minutes)

Memorize these words and then test yourself.

le football/rugby *luh futbohl/roogbee*	football/rugby
le tennis *luh tenees*	tennis
la natation *lah natasyoñ*	swimming
la voile *lah vwal*	sailing
la pêche *lah pesh*	fishing
la peinture *lah pañtyur*	painting
le vélo *luh vaylo*	cycling
la randonnée *lah rañdonay*	hiking

le bunker
luh bañkuh
bunker

le joueur de golf
luh joowur duh golf
golfer

Je joue au golf tout les jours.
juh joo oh golf too lay joor
I play golf every day.

3 **Useful phrases** (2 minutes)

Familiarize yourself with these phrases.

Je fais du rugby. *juh fay doo roogbee*	I play rugby.
Il joue au tennis. *eel joo oh tenees*	He plays tennis.
Elle fait de la peinture. *el fay duh lah pañtyur*	She paints.

4 Faire: to do or to make (4 minutes)

Il fait beau aujourd'hui.
eel fay boe oh-joordwee
It's nice weather today.

le drapeau
luh drapoh
flag

le parcours de golf
luh parkoor duh golf
golf course

The verb **faire** (*to do or to make*) is also used to describe the weather. Learn its different forms and practise the sample sentences below.

I do	**je fais** *juh fay*
you do (informal)	**tu fais** *tew fay*
he/she does	**il/elle fait** *eel/el fay*
we do	**nous faisons** *noo fayzon*
you do (formal/plural)	**vous faites** *voo fet*
they do	**ils/elles font** *eel/el foñ*
I go hiking.	**Je fais de la randonnée.** *juh fay duh lah rañdonay*
What do you do?	**Que faites-vous?** *kuh fet voo*
We play tennis.	**Nous faisons du tennis.** *noo fayzon doo tenees*

5 Put into practice (3 minutes)

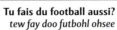

Practise these phrases. Then cover the text on the right and complete the dialogue in French. Check your answers.

Qu'est-ce que vous aimez faire?
keskuh voo zemay fair

What do you like doing?

Say: I like playing tennis.

J'aime jouer au tennis.
jem jooway oh tenees

Tu fais du football aussi?
tew fay doo futbohl ohsee

Do you play football as well?

Say: No. I play rugby.

Non, je fais du rugby.
noñ, juh fay doo roogbee

Cultural tip France boasts a huge variety of regional games, such as pelota in the Basque country. Most popular of all, the French version of bowls - **pétanque** or **boules** - is played in almost every town and village.

1 **Warm up** (1 minute)

Say "my husband" and "my wife". (pp.10-11)

How do you say "lunch" and "dinner" in French? (pp.20-1)

Say "Sorry, I'm busy". (pp.32-3)

VOIR DES GENS
Socializing

The French dinner table is the centre of their social world. You can expect to do a lot of your socializing enjoying food and wine. It is best to use the more polite **vous** form to talk to people you meet socially until they call you **tu**, in which case you can reciprocate.

l'invitée (f)
lanveetay
guest

2 **Useful phrases** (3 minutes)

Learn these phrases and then test yourself.

Je voudrais vous inviter à dîner. *juh voodray voo zaňveetay ah deenay*	I'd like to invite you for dinner.
Vous êtes libre mercredi prochain? *voo zet leebruh mairkrudee prochen*	Are you free next Wednesday?
Une autre fois peut-être. *oon awtruh fwah putetruh*	Another time perhaps.

Cultural tip When you go to someone's house for the first time, it is usual to bring flowers or wine. If you are invited again, having seen your host's house, you can bring something a little more personal.

3 **In conversation** (3 minutes)

Vous voulez venir dîner mardi?
voo voolay vuneer deenay mardee

Would you like to come to dinner on Tuesday?

Je suis désolée, je suis occupée.
juh swee dayzolay, juh swee zokoopay

I'm sorry, I'm busy.

Pourquoi pas jeudi?
poorkwah pah jurdee

What about Thursday?

4 Words to remember (3 minutes)

Familiarize yourself with these words and test yourself using the flap.

l'hôtesse (f)
lohtess
hostess

party	**la soirée** *lah swaray*
dinner party	**le dîner** *luh deenay*
invitation	**l'invitation** *lañveetasyoñ*
reception	**la réception** *lah raysepsyoñ*
cocktail party	**le cocktail** *luh koktail*

5 Put into practice (5 minutes)

Join in this conversation.

Vous pouvez venir à une réception ce soir.
voo poovay vuneer ah oon raysepsyoñ suh swah

Can you come to a reception this evening?

Say: Yes, I'd love to.

Oui, avec plaisir.
wee, avek playzeer

Ça commence à huit heures.
sah komoñs ah weet ur

It starts at eight o'clock.

Ask: Should I dress formally?

Il faut s'habiller?
eel foe sabeeyay

Merci de nous avoir invités.
mairsee duh noo zavwar añveetay
Thank you for inviting us.

Avec plaisir.
avek playzeer

With pleasure.

Venez avec votre mari.
vunay avek votruh maree

Please bring your husband.

Merci. A quelle heure?
mairsee. ah kel ur

Thank you. At what time?

Réponses
Answers (Cover with flap)

RÉVISEZ ET RÉPÉTEZ
Review and repeat

1 Animals

❶ **le poisson**
luh pwassoñ

❷ **l'oiseau**
lwazoe

❸ **le lapin**
luh lapañ

❹ **le chat**
luh shah

❺ **le hamster**
luh amstair

❻ **le chien**
luh shiañ

1 Animals (3 minutes)

Say the French words for the numbered animals.

rabbit ❸

❶ fish

hamster ❺

❹ cat

2 I like...

❶ **J'aime le rugby.**
jem luh roogbee

❷ **Je n'aime pas le golf.**
juh nem pah luh golf

❸ **J'aime faire de la peinture.**
jem fair duh lah pañtyur

❹ **Je n'aime pas jouer aux boules.**
juh nem pah jooway oh bool

2 I like... (4 minutes)

Say the following in French.

❶ I like rugby.
❷ I don't like golf.
❸ I like painting.
❹ I don't like playing boules.

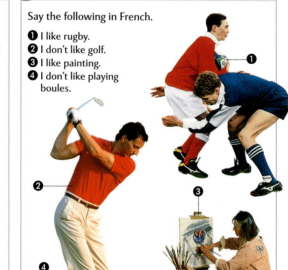

bird ❷

❻ dog

3 To do (4 minutes)

Use the correct form of the verb **faire** in these sentences.

❶ Tu _____ de la pêche?

❷ Elle _____ de la voile.

❸ Que _____ vous?

❹ Il _____ froid aujourd'hui.

❺ Vous _____ de la randonnée?

❻ J'aime _____ de la natation.

3 To do

❶ **fais**
fay

❷ **fait**
fay

❸ **faites**
fet

❹ **fait**
fay

❺ **faites**
fet

❻ **faire**
fair

4 An invitation (4 minutes)

You are invited for dinner. Join in the conversation, replying in French following the English prompts.

Vous voulez venir pour déjeuner vendredi?
❶ I'm sorry, I'm busy.

Pourquoi pas samedi?
❷ With pleasure.

Venez avec vos enfants.
❸ Thank you. At what time?

A douze heures et demie.
❹ That's good for me.

4 An invitation

❶ **Je suis désolé(e),
je suis occupé(e).**
*juh swee dayzolay,
juh swee zokoopay*

❷ **Avec plaisir.**
avek playzeer

❸ **Merci. A quelle
heure?**
mairsee, ah kel ur

❹ **C'est bon pour moi.**
say boñ poor mwah

Reinforce and progress

Regular practice is the key to maintaining and advancing your language skills. In this section you will find a variety of suggestions for reinforcing and extending your knowledge of French. Many involve returning to exercises in the book and using the dictionaries to extend their scope. Go back through the lessons in a different order, mix and match activities to make up your own 15-minute daily programme, or focus on topics that are of particular relevance to your current needs.

1   Warm up (1 minute)

Say "he is" and "they are". (pp.14–15)

Say "he is not" and "they are not". (pp.14–15)

What is French for "the children"? (pp.10–11)

Keep warmed up
Re-visit the Warm Up boxes to remind yourself of key words and phrases. Make sure you work your way through all of them on a regular basis.

3   I'd like... (3 minutes)

Say you'd like the following:

1 black coffee
jam **2**
bread **3**
large coffee **4** with milk

Review and repeat again
Work through a Review and Repeat lesson as a way of reinforcing words and phrases presented in the course. Return to the main lesson for any topic on which you are no longer confident.

3   In conversation: taxi (2 minutes)

Carry on conversing
Re-read the In Conversation panels. Say both parts of the conversation, paying attention to the pronunciation. Where possible, try incorporating new words from the dictionary.

Le marché aux fromages, s'il vous plaît.
luh marshayoe fromarj, seel voo play

The cheese market, please.

Oui, sans problème, monsieur.
wee. soñ problem musyuh

Yes, no problem, sir.

Vous pouvez me déposer ici, s'il vous plaît?
voo poovay muh dayposay eesee, seel voo play

Can you drop me here, please?

3   Useful phrases (5 minutes)

Familiarize yourself with these phrases and then test yourself.

The room is too cold/hot.	**La chambre est trop froide/chaude.** *lah shombruh ay troe fwrard/shohd*
There are no towels.	**Il n'y a pas de serviettes.** *eenyah pah duh survyet*
I need some soap.	**J'ai besoin de savon.** *jay buzwañ duh savoñ*
The shower doesn't work very well.	**La douche ne marche pas très bien.** *lah doosh nuh marsh pah tray byañ*

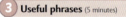

Practise phrases
Return to the Useful Phrases and Put into Practice exercises. Test yourself using the cover flap. When you are confident, devise your own versions of the phrases, using new words from the dictionary.

Match, repeat, and extend
Remind yourself of words related to specific topics
by returning to the Match and Repeat and Words to
Remember exercises. Test yourself using the cover flap.
Discover new words in that area by referring
to the dictionary and menu guide.

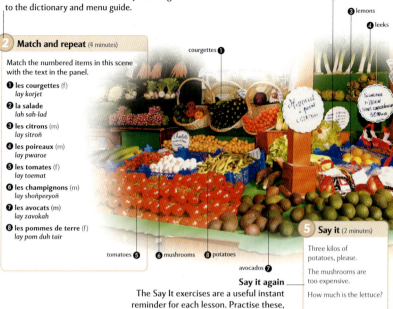

❷ lettuce
❸ lemons
❹ leeks
courgettes ❶

2 **Match and repeat** (4 minutes)

Match the numbered items in this scene
with the text in the panel.

❶ **les courgettes** (f)
lay korjet

❷ **la salade**
lah sah-lad

❸ **les citrons** (m)
lay sitroñ

❹ **les poireaux** (m)
lay pwaroe

❺ **les tomates** (f)
lay toemat

❻ **les champignons** (m)
lay shoñpeeyoñ

❼ **les avocats** (m)
lay zavokah

❽ **les pommes de terre** (f)
lay pom duh tair

tomatoes ❺   ❻ mushrooms   ❽ potatoes

avocados ❼

Say it again
The Say It exercises are a useful instant
reminder for each lesson. Practise these,
using your own vocabulary variations from
the dictionary or elsewhere in the lesson.

5 **Say it** (2 minutes)

Three kilos of
potatoes, please.

The mushrooms are
too expensive.

How much is the lettuce?

Using other resources

As well as working with this
book, try the following language
extension ideas:

Visit a French-speaking country and
try out your new skills with native
speakers. Find out if there is a French
community near you. There may be
shops, cafés, restaurants, and clubs.
Try to visit some of these and use
your French to order food and drink
and strike up conversations. Most
native speakers will be happy to
speak French to you.

Join a language class or club. There
are usually evening and day classes
available at a variety of different levels.
Or you could start a club yourself if you
have friends who are also interested in
keeping up their French.

Look at French magazines and
newspapers. The pictures will help you
to understand the text. Advertisements
are also a useful way of expanding
your vocabulary.

Use the Internet, where you can find
all kinds of websites for learning
languages, some of which offer free
online help and activities. You can also
find French websites for everything
from renting a house to shampooing
your pet. You can even access French
radio and TV stations online. Start by
going to a French search engine, such as
voila.fr, and key a subject that interests
you, or set yourself a challenge, for
example, finding a two-bedroom house
for rent by the sea in Normandy.

MENU GUIDE

This guide lists the most common terms you may encounter on French menus or when shopping for food. If you can't find an exact phrase, try looking up its component parts.

A

abats *offal*
abricot *apricot*
à emporter *to take away*
agneau *lamb*
aiguillette de bœuf *slices of rump steak*
ail *garlic*
ailloli *garlic mayonnaise*
à la broche *spit roast*
à la jardinière *with assorted vegetables*
à la normande *in cream sauce*
à la vapeur *steamed*
amande *almond*
ananas *pineapple*
anchois *anchovies*
andouillette *intestine sausage*
anguille *eel*
à point *medium*
artichaut *artichoke*
asperge *asparagus*
assiette anglaise *selection of cold meats*
au gratin *baked in a milk, cream, and cheese sauce*
au vin blanc *in white wine*
avocat *avocado*

B

banane *banana*
barbue *brill (fish)*
bavaroise *light mousse*
béarnaise *with béarnaise sauce*
bécasse *woodcock*
béchamel *white sauce*
beignet *fritter, doughnut*
beignet aux pommes *apple fritter*
betterave *beetroot*
beurre *butter*
beurre d'anchois *anchovy paste*
beurre noir *dark, melted butter*
bien cuit *well done*
bière *beer*
bière à la pression *draught beer*
bière blonde *lager*
bière brune *bitter beer*
bière panachée *shandy*

bifteck *steak*
bisque d'écrevisses *crayfish soup*
bisque de homard *lobster soup*
biscuit de Savoie *sponge cake*
blanquette de veau *veal stew*
bleu *very rare*
bleu d'auvergne *blue cheese from Auvergne*
bœuf bourguignon *beef cooked in red wine*
bœuf braisé *braised beef*
bœuf en daube *beef casserole*
bœuf miroton *beef and onion stew*
bœuf mode *beef stew with carrots*
bolet *boletus (mushroom)*
boudin blanc *white pudding*
boudin noir *black pudding*
bouillabaisse *fish soup*
bouilli *boiled*
bouillon *broth*
bouillon de légumes *vegetable stock*
bouillon de poule *chicken stock*
boulette *meatball*
bouquet rose *prawns*
bourride *fish soup*
brandade *cod in cream and garlic*
brioche *round roll*
brochet *pike*
brochette *kebab*
brugnon *nectarine*
brûlot *flambéed brandy*
brut *very dry*

C

cabillaud *cod*
café *coffee (black)*
café au lait *white coffee*
café complet *continental breakfast*
café crème *white coffee*
café glacé *iced coffee*
café liégeois *iced coffee with cream*
caille *quail*
calamar/calmar *squid*
calvados *apple brandy*

canapé *small open sandwich, canapé*
canard *duck*
canard laqué *Peking duck*
caneton *duckling*
cantal *white cheese from Auvergne*
câpres *capers*
carbonnade *beef cooked in beer*
cari *curry*
carotte *carrot*
carottes Vichy *carrots in butter and parsley*
carpe *carp*
carré d'agneau *rack of lamb*
carrelet *plaice*
carte *menu*
carte des vins *wine list*
casse-croûte *snacks*
cassis *blackcurrant*
cassoulet *bean, pork and duck casserole*
céleri/céleri rave *celeriac*
céleri en branches *celery*
cèpe *cep (mushroom)*
cerise *cherry*
cerises à l'eau de vie *cherries in brandy*
cervelle *brains*
chabichou *goat's and cow's milk cheese*
chablis *dry white wine from Burgundy*
champignon *mushroom*
champignon de Paris *white button mushroom*
chanterelle *chanterelle (mushroom)*
chantilly *whipped cream*
charcuterie *sausages, ham and pâtés; pork products*
charlotte *dessert with fruit, cream, and biscuits*
chausson aux pommes *apple turnover*
cheval *horse*
chèvre *goat's cheese*
chevreuil *venison*
chicorée *endive*
chocolat chaud *hot chocolate*
chocolat glacé *iced chocolate*
chou *cabbage*

chou à la crème *cream puff*
choucroute *sauerkraut with sausages and ham*
chou-fleur *cauliflower*
chou rouge *red cabbage*
choux de Bruxelles *Brussels sprouts*
cidre *cider*
cidre doux *sweet cider*
citron *lemon*
citron pressé *fresh lemon juice*
civet de lièvre *jugged hare*
clafoutis *baked batter pudding with fruit*
cochon de lait *suckling pig*
cocktail de crevettes *prawn cocktail*
cœur *heart*
coing *quince*
colin *hake*
compote *stewed fruit*
comté *hard cheese from the Jura*
concombre *cucumber*
confit de canard *duck preserved in fat*
confit d'oie *goose preserved in fat*
confiture *jam*
congre *conger eel*
consommé *clear meat or chicken soup*
coq au vin *chicken in red wine*
coque *cockle*
coquelet *cockerel*
coquilles Saint-Jacques *scallops in cream sauce*
côte de porc *pork chop*
côtelette *chop*
cotriade bretonne *fish soup from Brittany*
coulommiers *rich, soft cheese*
court-bouillon *stock*
crabe *crab*
crème *cream; creamy sauce or dessert; white (coffee)*
crème à la vanille *vanilla custard*
crème anglaise *custard*
crème chantilly *whipped cream*
crème d'asperges *cream of asparagus soup*
crème de bolets *cream of mushroom soup*
crème de volaille *cream of chicken soup*
crème d'huîtres *cream of oyster soup*
crème fouettée *whipped cream*
crème pâtissière *rich, creamy custard*
crème renversée *set custard*
crème vichyssoise *cold leek and potato soup*

crêpe *pancake*
crêpe à la crème de marron *pancake with chestnut cream*
crêpe à l'œuf *pancake with fried egg*
crêpe de froment *wheat pancake*
crêpes Suzette *pancakes flambéed with orange sauce*
crépinette *small sausage patty wrapped in fat*
cresson *cress*
crevette grise *shrimp*
crevette rose *prawn*
croque-madame *grilled cheese and ham sandwich with a fried egg*
croque-monsieur *grilled cheese and ham sandwich*
crottin de Chavignol *small goat's cheese*
crustacés *shellfish*
cuisses de grenouille *frogs' legs*

D

dartois *pastry with jam*
dégustation *wine tasting*
digestif *liqueur*
dinde *turkey*
doux *sweet*

E

eau minérale gazeuse *sparkling mineral water*
eau minérale plate *still mineral water*
échalote *shallot*
écrevisse *freshwater crayfish*
endive *chicory*
en papillote *baked in foil or paper*
entrecôte *rib steak*
entrecôte au poivre *peppered rib steak*
entrecôte maître d'hôtel *steak with butter and parsley*
entrée *starter*
entremets *dessert*
épaule d'agneau farcie *stuffed shoulder of lamb*
épinards en branches *leaf spinach*
escalope de veau milanaise *veal escalope with tomato sauce*
escalope panée *breaded escalope*
escargot *snail*
estouffade de bœuf *beef casserole*
estragon *tarragon*

F

faisan *pheasant*
farci *stuffed*
fenouil *fennel*
filet *fillet*
filet de bœuf Rossini *fillet of beef with foie gras*
filet de perche *perch fillet*
fine *fine brandy*
flageolets *kidney beans*
flan *custard tart*
foie de veau *veal liver*
foie gras *goose or duck liver preserve*
foies de volaille *chicken livers*
fonds d'artichaut *artichoke hearts*
fondue bourguignonne *meat fondue*
fondue savoyarde *cheese fondue*
fraise *strawberry*
fraise des bois *wild strawberry*
framboise *raspberry*
frisée *curly lettuce*
frit *deep-fried*
frites *chips*
fromage *cheese*
fromage blanc *cream cheese*
fromage de chèvre *goat's cheese*
fruits de mer *seafood*

G

galette *round, flat cake or savoury wholemeal crêpe*
garni *with potatoes and vegetables*
gâteau *cake*
gaufre *wafer; waffle*
gelée *jelly*
Gewürztraminer *dry white wine from Alsace*
gibier *game*
gigot d'agneau *leg of lamb*
girolle *chanterelle (mushroom)*
glace *ice cream*
goujon *gudgeon (fish)*
gratin *dish baked with milk, cheese, and cream*
gratin dauphinois *sliced potatoes baked in milk, cream, and cheese*
gratinée *baked onion soup*
grillé *grilled*
grondin *gurnard (fish)*
groseille rouge *redcurrant*

H

hachis parmentier *shepherd's pie*
hareng mariné *marinated herring*
haricots *beans*

haricots blancs *haricot beans*
haricots verts *green beans*
homard *lobster*
hors-d'œuvre *starter*
huître *oyster*

I, J

îles flottantes *floating islands* (soft meringue on custard)
infusion *herb tea*
jambon *ham*
jambon de Bayonne *smoked and cured ham*
julienne *soup with chopped vegetables*
jus de fruits *fruit juice*
jus de pomme *apple juice*
jus d'orange *orange juice*

K, L

kir *white wine with blackcurrant liqueur*
kirsch *cherry brandy*
lait *milk*
laitue *lettuce*
langouste *saltwater crayfish*
langoustine *Dublin Bay prawn*
lapereau *young rabbit*
lapin *rabbit*
lapin de garenne *wild rabbit*
lard *bacon*
légume *vegetable*
lentilles *lentils*
lièvre *hare*
limande *lemon sole*
livarot *strong, soft cheese from the north of France*
longe *loin*
lotte *monkfish*
loup au fenouil *bass with fenne*

M

macédoine de légumes *mixed vegetables*
mache *corn salad (leafy vegetable)*
mangue *mango*
maquereau *mackerel*
marc *grape brandy*
marcassin *young boar*
marchand de vin *in red wine sauce*
marron *chestnut*
massepain *marzipan*
menthe *peppermint*
menthe à l'eau *mint cordial with water*
menu du jour *today's menu*
menu gastronomique *gourmet menu*
menu touristique *tourist menu*

merlan *whiting*
millefeuille *custard slice*
millésime *vintage*
morille *morel (mushroom)*
morue *cod*
moules *mussels*
moules marinière *mussels in white wine*
mousseux *sparkling*
moutarde *mustard*
mouton *mutton*
mulet *mullet*
munster *strong cheese*
mûre *blackberry*
Muscadet *dry white wine*
myrtille *bilberry*

N

nature *plain*
navarin *mutton stew with vegetables*
navet *turnip*
noisette *hazelnut*
noisette d'agneau *medallion of lamb*
noix *nuts, walnuts*
nouilles *noodles*

O

œuf à la coque *boiled egg*
œuf dur *hard-boiled egg*
œuf mollet *soft-boiled egg*
œuf poché *poached egg*
œufs brouillés *scrambled eggs*
œuf sur le plat *fried egg*
oie *goose*
oignon *onion*
omelette au naturel *plain omelette*
omelette aux fines herbes *herb omelette*
omelette paysanne *omelette with potatoes and bacon*
orange pressée *fresh orange juice*
oseille *sorrel*
oursin *sea urchin*

P

pain *bread*
pain au chocolat *chocolate croissant*
palette de porc *shoulder of pork*
palourde *clam*
pamplemousse *grapefruit*
pastis *anise-flavoured alcoholic drink*
pâté de canard *duck pâté*
pâté de foie de volaille *chicken liver pâté*
pâte feuilletée *puff pastry*

pâtes *pasta*
pêche *peach*
perdreau *young partridge*
perdrix *partridge*
petite friture *whitebait*
petit pain *roll*
petit pois *peas*
petits fours *small pastries*
petit suisse *cream cheese*
pied de porc *pig's feet*
pigeonneau *young pigeon*
pignatelle *cheese fritter*
pilaf de mouton *rice dish with mutton*
pintade *guinea fowl*
piperade *dish of egg, tomatoes, and peppers*
pissaladière *Provençal dish similar to pizza*
pistache *pistachio*
plat du jour *dish of the day*
plateau de fromages *cheese board*
pochouse *fish casserole with white wine*
poire *pear*
poireau *leek*
poisson *fish*
poivre *pepper*
poivron *red/green pepper*
pomme *apple*
pomme de terre *potato*
pommes de terre à l'anglaise *boiled potatoes*
pommes de terre en robe de chambre/des champs *baked potatoes*
pommes de terre sautées *fried potatoes*
pommes frites *chips*
pommes paille *finely cut chips*
pommes vapeur *steamed potatoes*
porc *pork*
potage *soup*
potage bilibi *fish and oyster soup*
potage Crécy *carrot and rice soup*
potage cressonnière *watercress soup*
potage Esaü *lentil soup*
potage parmentier *leek and potato soup*
potage printanier *vegetable soup*
potage Saint-Germain *split pea soup*
potage velouté *creamy soup*
pot-au-feu *beef and vegetable stew*
potée *vegetable and meat stew*
Pouilly-Fuissé *dry white wine from Burgundy*
poule au pot *chicken and vegetable stew*

poulet basquaise *chicken with ratatouille*
poulet chasseur *chicken with mushrooms and white wine*
poulet créole *chicken in white sauce with rice*
poulet rôti *roast chicken*
praire *clam*
provençale *with tomatoes, garlic and herbs*
prune *plum*
pruneau *prune*
pudding *plum pudding*
purée *mashed potatoes*

Q

quenelle *meat or fish dumpling*
queue de bœuf *oxtail*
quiche lorraine *egg, bacon, and cream tart*

R

raclette *Swiss dish of melted cheese*
radis *radish*
ragoût *stew*
raie *skate*
raie au beurre noir *skate fried in butter*
raifort *horseradish*
raisin *grape*
râpé *grated*
rascasse *scorpion fish*
ratatouille *stew of peppers, courgettes, aubergines, and tomatoes*
ravigote *herb dressing*
reblochon *strong cheese from Savoy*
rémoulade *mayonnaise dressing with herbs, mustard, and capers*
rigotte *small goat's cheese from Lyon*
rillettes *potted pork or goose meat*
ris de veau *veal sweetbread*
riz *rice*
riz pilaf *spicy rice with meat or seafood*
rognon *kidney*
roquefort *blue cheese*
rôti *roasted/joint of meat*
rouget *mullet*

S

sabayon *zabaglione (whipped egg yolk in Marsala wine)*
sablé *shortbread*
saignant *rare*
saint-honoré *cream puff cake*
saint-marcellin *goat's cheese*

salade composée *mixed salad*
salade russe *diced vegetables in mayonnaise*
salade verte *green salad*
salmis *game stew*
salsifis *oyster plant, salsify*
sanglier *wild boar*
sauce aurore *white sauce with tomato purée*
sauce béarnaise *thick sauce of eggs and butter*
sauce blanche *white sauce*
sauce gribiche *dressing with hard-boiled eggs*
sauce hollandaise *rich sauce of eggs, butter and vinegar, served with fish*
sauce Madère *Madeira sauce*
sauce matelote *wine sauce*
sauce Mornay *béchamel sauce with cheese*
sauce mousseline *hollandaise sauce with cream*
sauce poulette *sauce of mushrooms and egg yolks*
sauce ravigote *dressing with shallots and herbs*
sauce suprême *creamy sauce*
sauce tartare *mayonnaise with herbs and gherkins*
sauce veloutée *white sauce with egg yolks and cream*
sauce vinot *wine sauce*
saucisse *sausage*
saucisse de Francfort *frankfurter*
saucisse de Strasbourg *beef sausage*
saucisson *salami*
saumon *salmon*
saumon fumé *smoked salmon*
sauternes *sweet white wine*
savarin *rum baba*
sec *dry*
seiche *cuttlefish*
sel *salt*
service (non) compris *service (not) included*
service 12% inclus *12% service charge included*
sole bonne femme *sole in white wine and mushrooms*
sole meunière *floured sole fried in butter*
soupe *soup*
soupe au pistou *thick vegetable soup with basil*
steak au poivre *peppered steak*
steak frites *steak and chips*
steak haché *minced meat, minced beef*
steak tartare *raw minced beef with a raw egg*
sucre *sugar*

suprême de volaille *chicken in cream sauce*

T

tanche *tench (fish)*
tarte aux fraises *strawberry tart*
tarte aux pommes *apple tart*
tarte frangipane *almond cream tart*
tartelette *small tart*
tarte Tatin *baked apple dish*
tartine *bread and butter*
tendrons de veau *breast of veal*
terrine *pâté*
tête de veau *calf's head*
thé *tea*
thé à la menthe *mint tea*
thé au lait *tea with milk*
thé citron *lemon tea*
thon *tuna*
tomates farcies *stuffed tomatoes*
tome de Savoie *white cheese from Savoy*
tournedos *round beef steak*
tourte *covered pie*
tourteau *type of crab*
tripes à la mode de Caen *tripe in spicy vegetable sauce*
truite au bleu *poached trout*
truite aux amandes *trout with almonds*
truite meunière *trout in flour and fried in butte*

V, Y

vacherin *strong, soft cheese from the Jura*
vacherin glacé *ice cream meringue*
veau *veal*
velouté de tomate *cream of tomato soup*
vermicelle *vermicelli (very fine pasta)*
viande *meat*
vin *wine*
vinaigrette *French dressing*
vin blanc *white wine*
vin de pays *local wine*
vin de table *table wine*
vin rosé *rosé wine*
vin rouge *red wine*
volaille *poultry*
VSOP *mature brandy*
yaourt *yoghurt*

DICTIONARY
English to French

The gender of a singular French noun is indicated by the word for *the*: **le** and **la** (masculine and feminine). If these are abbreviated to **l'** in front of a vowel or the letter *h*, or if the noun is plural, indicated by **les,** then the gender is indicated by the abbreviations (m) or (f). French adjectives (adj) vary according to the gender and number of the word they describe; the masculine form is shown here. In most cases, you add an **-e** to the masculine form to make it feminine. Certain endings use a different rule: masculine adjectives that end in **-x** adopt an **-se** ending in the feminine form, while those that end in **-ien** change to **-ienne**. Some feminine adjectives that do not follow these rules are shown here and follow the abbreviation (fem). For the plural form, a (silent) **-s** is usually added.

A

a **un/une**
about: about sixteen **environ seize**
accelerator **l'accélérateur** (m)
accident **l'accident** (m)
accommodation **l'hébergement** (m)
accountant **le/la comptable**
ache **la douleur**
adaptor (plug) **la prise multiple;** (voltage) **l'adaptateur** (m)
address **l'adresse** (f)
adhesive **l'adhésif** (m)
admission charge **le prix d'entrée**
advance **l'avance** (f)
after **après**
afternoon **l'après-midi** (m)
aftershave **l'après-rasage** (m)
again **de nouveau**
against **contre**
agenda **l'ordre du jour** (m)
agent **l'agent** (m)
AIDS **SIDA**
air **l'air** (m)
air conditioning **la climatisation**
aircraft **l'avion** (m)
airline **la compagnie aérienne**
air mail **par avion**
air mattress **le matelas pneumatique**
airport **l'aéroport** (m)
airport bus **la navette (pour l'aéroport)**
aisle (supermarket) **rayon**
alarm clock **le réveil**
alcohol **l'alcool** (m)
Algeria **l'Algérie** (f)

Algerian **algérien(ne)**
all **tout;** *all the streets* **toutes les rues;** *that's all* **c'est tout**
allergic **allergique**
almost **presque**
alone **seul**
Alps **les Alpes** (f)
already **déjà**
always **toujours**
am: I am **je suis**
ambulance **l'ambulance** (f)
America **l'Amérique** (f)
American **américain(e)**
and **et**
Andorra **Andorre**
ankle **la cheville**
another (different) **un/une autre;** *another coffee, please* **encore un café, s'il vous plaît**
answering machine **le réponder**
antifreeze **l'antigel** (m)
antique shop **le magasin d'antiquités; l'antiquaire** (m)
antiseptic **l'antiseptique** (m)
apartment **l'appartement** (m)
aperitif **l'apéritif** (m)
appetite **l'appétit** (m)
apple **la pomme**
application form **le formulaire de demande**
appointment **le rendez-vous**
apricot **l'abricot** (m)
April **avril**
architecture **l'architecture** (f)
are: you are (singular informal) **tu es;** *we are* **nous sommes;** (plural; singular formal) **vous êtes;** *they are* **ils/elles sont**

arm **le bras**
armchair **le fauteuil**
arrival **l'arrivée** (f)
arrive **arriver**
art **l'art** (m)
art gallery **le musée d'art; la galerie d'art**
artist **l'artiste** (m)
as: as soon as possible **dès que possible**
ashtray **le cendrier**
asleep **endormi;** *he's asleep* **il dort**
aspirin **l'aspirine** (f)
asthmatic **asthmatique**
at: at the post office **à la poste;** *at the café* **au café;** *at 3 o'clock* **à 3 heures**
attic **le grenier**
attractive **attirant**
August **août**
aunt **la tante**
Australia **l'Australie** (f)
Australian **australien(ne)**
automatic **automatique**
autumn **l'automne** (m)
avocado **l'avocat** (m)
away: is it far away? **est-ce que c'est loin?;** *go away!* **allez-vous en!**
awful **affreux**
axe **la hache**
axle **l'essieu** (m)

B

baby **le bébé**
baby wipes **les lingettes** (f)
back (not front) **l'arrière** (m); (body) **le dos;** *I'll come back tomorrow* **je reviendrai demain**
backpack **le sac à dos**

bacon **le bacon;** *bacon and eggs* **des œufs au bacon**
bad **mauvais**
baggage **les bagages** (m)
baggage check in **l'enregistrement des bagages** (m)
baggage claim **la réclamation de bagages**
bait **l'appât** (m)
bake **cuire**
bakery **la boulangerie**
balcony **le balcon**
bald **chauve**
ball (football etc) **le ballon;** (tennis etc) **la balle**
ballpoint pen **le stylo-bille**
banana **la banane**
band (musicians) **le groupe**
bandage **le pansement, le bandage**
bank **la banque**
banknote **le billet**
bar **le bar;**
barbecue **le barbecue**
barber's **le coiffeur**
bargain **la affaire**
basement **le sous-sol**
basin (sink) **le lavabo**
basket **le panier**
bath **le bain;** (bathtub) **la baignoire;** *to have a bath* **prendre un bain**
bathroom **la salle de bains**
battery (car) **la batterie;** (torch) **la pile**
be **être**
beach **la plage**
beans **les haricots** (m)
beard **la barbe**
beautiful **beau,** (fem) **belle**
because **parce que**
bed **le lit**
bed linen **les draps** (m)
bedroom **la chambre**
beef **le bœuf**
beer **la bière**
before **avant**
beginner **le débutant, la débutante**
beginners' slope **la piste pour débutants**
behind **derrière**
beige **beige**
Belgian **belge**
Belgium **la Belgique**
bell (church) **la cloche;** (door) **la sonnette**
below ... **sous ...**
belt **la ceinture**
beside **à côté de**

best: the best **le meilleur**
better **mieux**
between ... **entre ...**
bicycle **la bicyclette, le vélo**
big **grand**
bill **l'addition** (f)
bin liner **le sac poubelle**
bird **l'oiseau** (m)
birthday **l'anniversaire** (m); *happy birthday!* **joyeux anniversaire!**
biscuit **le biscuit**
bite (by dog) **la morsure;** (by snake) **la piqûre,** (verb: dog) insect; **mordre;** (insect, snake) **piquer**
bitter **amer**
black **noir**
blackberry **la mûre**
blackcurrant **le cassis**
blanket **la couverture**
bleach **l'eau de Javel** (f); (verb) **décolorer**
blind (cannot see) **aveugle;** (window) **le store**
blister **l'ampoule** (f)
blizzard **la tempête de neige**
blond (adj) **blond**
blood **le sang**
blood test **la prise de sang**
blouse **le chemisier**
blue **bleu**
boarding pass **la carte d'embarquement**
boat **le bateau;** (smaller) **la barque**
body **le corps**
boil (verb) **bouillir**
boiled **bouilli**
boiler **le chauffe-eau**
bolt (on door) **le verrou;** **verrouiller** (verb)
bone **l'os** (m); (fish) **l'arête** (f)
bonnet (car) **le capot**
book **le livre; réserver** (verb)
bookshop **la librairie**
boot (footwear) **la botte;** (car) **le coffre**
border **la frontière**
boring **ennuyeux**
born: I was born in ... **je suis né(e) en ...**
both **les deux;** *both of them* **tous les deux;** *both of us* **nous deux;** *both large and small* **grand et petit à la fois**
bottle **la bouteille**
bottle opener **le décapsuleur, l'ouvre-bouteille** (m)

bottom **le fond;** (part of body) **le derrière**
bowl **le bol;** (animal) **la gamelle**
box **la boîte**
box office (theatre etc) **le bureau de location**
boy **le garçon**
boyfriend **le petit ami**
bra **le soutien-gorge**
bracelet **le bracelet**
braces (clothes) **les bretelles** (f)
brake **le frein;** (verb) **freiner**
branch **la branche**
brandy **le cognac**
bread **le pain**
breakdown (car) **la panne;** (nervous) **la dépression;** *I've had a breakdown* (car) **je suis tombé en panne**
breakfast **le petit déjeuner**
breathe **respirer**
bricklayer **le maçon**
bridge **le pont**
briefcase **l'attaché-case** (m)
British **britannique**
Brittany **la Bretagne**
brochure **la brochure**
broken **cassé;** *broken leg* **la jambe cassée;** *broken down* **en panne**
brooch **la broche**
brother **le frère**
brown **marron**
bruise **le bleu**
brush **la brosse;** (paintbrush) **le pinceau;** (broom) **le balai;** (verb) **brosser**
Brussels **Bruxelles**
bucket **le seau**
budget **le budget**
builder **le constructeur**
building **le bâtiment**
bumper **le pare-chocs**
bunker **le bunker**
burglary **le cambriolage**
burn **la brûlure;** (verb) **brûler**
bus **le bus**
business **les affaires** (f); *it's none of your business* **cela ne vous regarde pas**
business card **la carte de visite**
bus station **la gare routière**
bus stop **l'arrêt de bus** (m)
busy (occupied) **occupé;** (street) **animé**
but **mais**
butcher's **la boucherie**
butter **le beurre**

button **le bouton**
buy **acheter**
by: by the window **près de la fenêtre; *by Friday* d'ici vendredi; *by myself* tout seul; *written by* écrit par**

C

cabbage **le chou**
cabinet **le placard**
cable car **le téléphérique**
cable TV **la télé cablée**
café **le café**
cage **la cage**
cake **le gâteau**
cake shop **la pâtisserie**
calculator **la calculette**
call: what's it called? **comment est-ce que ça s'appelle?**
camcorder **le caméscope**
camera **l'appareil-photo (m)**
camper van **le camping-car**
campfire **le feu de camp**
campsite **le terrain de camping**
camshaft **l'arbre à cames (m)**
can (vessel) **la boîte de conserve; (to be able) pouvoir; *can I have ...?* Je peux avoir ...?; *can you ...?* Vous pouvez ...?**
Canada **le Canada**
Canadian **canadien(ne)**
canal **le canal**
candle **la bougie**
canoe **le canoë**
can opener **l'ouvre-boîte (m)**
cap (hat) **la casquette; (bottle) la capsule**
car **la voiture; (train) la voiture, le wagon**
caravan **la caravane**
carburettor **le carburateur**
card **la carte**
cardigan **le gilet**
careful **prudent; *careful!* attention!; *be careful!* soyez prudent!**
caretaker **le/la concierge**
car park **le parking**
carpenter **le charpentier**
carpet **le tapis**
carriage (train) **la voiture**
carrot **la carotte**
car seat (for a baby) **le siège pour bébé**
case **la valise**
cash **l'argent (m); *to pay cash* payer en liquide**

cashier **le guichet**
cash machine **le distributeur automatique**
cassette **la cassette**
cassette player **le lecteur de cassettes**
castle **le château**
cat **le chat**
cathedral **la cathédrale**
cauliflower **le chou-fleur**
cave **la grotte**
ceiling **le plafond**
cellar **la cave**
cemetery **le cimetière**
central heating **le chauffage central**
centre **le centre**
certificate **le certificat**
chair **la chaise**
change (money) **la monnaie; (verb: money) changer; (clothes) se changer**
Channel **la Manche**
Channel Islands **les îles Anglo-Normandes**
Channel Tunnel **le tunnel sous la Manche**
charger **le chargeur**
cheap **bon marché, pas cher**
check-in **l'enregistrement (m)**
check in **faire enregistrer ses bagages**
check-out (supermarket) **la caisse**
cheers! (toast) **santé!**
cheese **le fromage**
cheese shop **la fromagerie**
chemist's **la pharmacie**
cheque **le chèque**
chequebook **le carnet de chèques**
cherry **la cerise**
chess **les échecs (m)**
chest **la poitrine**
chest of drawers **la commode**
chicken **le poulet**
child **l'enfant (m)**
children **les enfants (m)**
children's ward **le service de pédiatrie**
chimney **la cheminée**
china **la porcelaine**
chips **les frites (f)**
chocolate **le chocolat; *a box of chocolates* la boîte de chocolats; *chocolate bar* la tablette de chocolat**
chop (food) **la côtelette; (verb: cut) couper**
church **l'église (f)**

cigar **le cigare**
cigarette **la cigarette**
cinema **le cinéma**
city **la ville**
city centre **le centre ville**
class **la classe**
classical music **la musique classique**
clean (adj) **propre**
cleaner **la femme de ménages**
clear **clair**
clever **intelligent**
clock **l'horloge (f), la pendule**
close **près (near); étouffant (stuffy); fermer (verb)**
closed **fermé**
clothes **les vêtements (m)**
clubs (cards) **trèfle**
clutch **l'embrayage (m)**
coat **le manteau**
coat hanger **le cintre**
cockroach **le cafard**
cocktail party **le cocktail**
coffee **le café; *white coffee* café crème**
coin **la pièce**
cold (illness) **le rhume; froid (adj)**
collar **le col, le collier**
collection (stamps etc) **la collection; (postal) la levée**
colour **la couleur**
colour film **la pellicule couleur**
comb **le peigne; (verb) peigner**
come **venir; *I come from ...* je viens de ...; *we came last week* nous sommes arrivés la semaine dernière**
compact disc **le disque compact**
company **la compagnie**
compartment **le compartiment**
complicated **compliqué**
computer **l'ordinateur (m)**
computer games **les jeux vidéos (m)**
concert **le concert**
conditioner (hair) **le baume après-shampooing**
condom **le préservatif**
conductor (orchestra) **le chef d'orchestre**
confectioner **le confiseur**
conference **la conférence**

conference room **la salle de conférences**
congratulations! **félicitations!**
consulate **le consulat**
consultant **consultant(e)**
contact lenses **les verres de contact** (f)
contraceptive **le contraceptif**
cook **le cuisinier; faire la cuisine** (verb)
cooker **la cuisinière**
cooking utensils **les utensiles de cuisine** (f)
cool **frais,** (fem) **fraîche**
cork **le bouchon**
corkscrew **le tire-bouchon**
corner **le coin**
corridor **le couloir**
Corsica **la Corse**
Corsican **corse**
cosmetics **les produits de beauté** (m)
cost (verb) **coûter;** *how much does it cost?* **combien ça coûte?**
cot **le lit d'enfant**
cotton **le coton**
cotton balls **le coton hydrophile**
cough **la toux;** (verb) **tousser**
country (state) **le pays;** (not town) **la campagne**
courgette **la courgette**
cousin **le cousin**
crab **le crabe**
cramp **la crampe**
crayfish (freshwater) **l'écrevisse** (f); (saltwater) **la langouste**
cream **la crème**
credit card **la carte de crédit**
crisps **les chips** (f)
cross over (verb) **traverser**
crowded **bondé**
cruise **la croisière**
crutches **les béquilles** (f)
cry (weep) **pleurer;** (shout) **crier**
cucumber **le concombre**
cuff links **les boutons de manchette** (m)
cup **la tasse**
curlers **les rouleaux** (m)
curls **les boucles** (f)
current **le courant**
curry **le curry**
curtain **le rideau**
customs **la douane**
cut **la coupure;** (verb) **couper**
cycling **le vélo**

D

dad **papa**
dairy products **les produits laitiers** (m)
dance **la danse;** (verb) **danser**
dangerous **dangereux**
dark **foncé;** *dark blue* **bleu foncé**
daughter **la fille**
day **le jour**
dead **mort**
deaf **sourd**
dear **cher**
debit card **la carte bancaire**
December **décembre**
decorator **le décorateur**
deep **profond**
delay **le retard**
deliberately **exprès**
delicatessen **la charcuterie**
delivery **la livraison**
dentist **le/la dentiste**
dentures **le dentier**
deny **nier**
deodorant **le déodorant**
department **la département**
department store **le grand magasin**
departures (airport etc) **le départ**
designer **le designer**
desk **le bureau**
desserts **les desserts** (m)
develop **développer**
diabetic **diabétique**
diamond (jewel) **le diamant**
diamonds (cards) **carreau**
diarrhoea **la diarrhée**
diary **l'agenda** (m)
dictionary **le dictionnaire**
die **mourir**
diesel **le diesel; le gazoile**
different **différent;** *that's different* **c'est différent;** *I'd like a different one* **j'en voudrais un autre**
difficult **difficile**
dining room **la salle à manger**
dinner **le dîner**
dinner party **le dîner**
directory (telephone) **l'annuaire** (m); **les reseignments** (m)
disabled **handicapé**
disco **le discothèque**
discount **la réduction**
dish cloth **le torchon**
dishwasher **le lave-vaisselle**
disposable nappies **les couches à jeter** (f)

distributor (car) **le delco**
dive (verb) **plonger**
diving board **le plongeoir**
divorced **divorcé**
do **faire;** *how do you do?* **comment allez-vous?**
dock **le quai**
doctor **le docteur; médecin**
document **le document**
dog **le chien**
doll **la poupée**
dollar **le dollar**
door (building) **la porte;** (car) **la portière**
double room **la chambre pour deux personnes**
doughnut **le beignet**
down **en bas**
drawer **le tiroir**
drawing pin **la punaise**
dress **la robe**
drink **la boisson;** (verb) **boire;** *would you like a drink?* **vous voulez boire quelque chose?**
drinking water **l'eau potable** (f)
drive (verb: car) **conduire**
driver **le conducteur**
driveway **le passage**
driving licence **le permis de conduire**
drops **les goutes** (f)
drunk **soûl, ivre**
dry **sec,** (fem) **sèche**
dry cleaner's **le pressing**
during **pendant**
duster **le chiffon à poussière**
duty-free **hors-taxe**
duvet **la couette**

E

each (every) **chaque;** *two euros each* **deux euros pièce**
ear **l'oreille** (f)
early **tôt**
earrings **les boucles d'oreille** (f)
east **l'est** (m)
easy **facile**
eat **manger**
egg **l'œuf** (m)
eight **huit**
eighteen **dix-huit**
eighty **quatre-vingt**
either: *either of them* **n'importe lequel;** *either ... or ...* **soit ... soit ...**
elastic **élastique**
elastic band **l'élastique** (m)

elbow le coude
electric électrique
electrician électricien(ne)
electricity l'électricité (f)
eleven onze
else: something else autre
    chose; someone else
    quelqu'un d'autre;
    somewhere else ailleurs
e-mail l'email (m), le
    message, la messagerie
    électronique
e-mail address l'adresse
    électronique (f)
embarrassing gênant
embassy l'ambassade (f)
embroidery la broderie
emerald l'émeraude (f)
emergency l'urgence (f)
emergency departement la
    salle des urgences
emergency exit la sortie de
    secours
empty vide
end la fin
engaged (couple) fiancé
engine (car) le moteur; (train)
    la locomotive
engineer l'ingénieur (m)
engineering l'ingénierie (f)
England l'Angleterre (f)
English anglais(e)
enlargement
    l'agrandissement (m)
enough assez
entertainment le
    divertissement
entrance l'entrée (f)
envelope l'enveloppe (f)
epileptic épileptique
eraser la gomme
escalator l'escalier roulant (m)
especially particulièrement
estimate l'estimation (f)
evening le soir
every chaque
everyone tout le monde
everything tout
everywhere partout
example l'exemple (m); for
    example par exemple
excellent excellent
excess baggage l'excédent de
    bagages (m)
exchange (verb) échanger
exchange rate le taux
    de change
excursion l'excursion (f)
excuse me! pardon!
executive (in company)
    cadre (m)

exhaust (car) le pot
    d'echappement
exhibition l'exposition (f)
exit la sortie
expensive cher
extension lead la rallonge
exterior l'extérieure (m);
    extérieure (adj)
eye l'œil (m)
eyebrow le sourcil
eyes les yeux (m)

F

face le visage
faint vague; to faint evanouir
fair la foire; (just) juste; it's
    not fair ce n'est pas juste
fan (ventilator) le
    ventilateur; (enthusiast)
    le/la fan
fan belt la courroie du
    ventilateur
fantastic fantastique
far loin; how far is it to ...?
    est-ce que ... est loin
    d'ici?
fare le prix du billet
farm la ferme
farmer le fermier
fashion la mode
fast rapide
fat (of person) gros, (fem)
    grosse; (on meat etc) le gras
father le père
February fevrier
feel (touch) toucher; I feel hot
    j'ai chaud; I feel like ... j'ai
    envie de ...; I don't feel well
    je ne me sens pas bien
feet les pieds (m)
felt-tip pen le feutre
ferry (small) le bac; (large)
    le ferry
fever la fièvre
fiancé le fiancé
fiancée la fiancée
field le champ; (academic)
    secteur (m)
fifteen quinze
fifty cinquante
fig la figue
figures les chiffres (m)
filling (in tooth) le plombage;
    (in sandwich, cake)
    la garniture
film le film
filter paper le papier filtre
finger le doigt
fire le feu; (blaze) l'incendie
    (m)

fire extinguisher l'extincteur
    (m)
fireplace la cheminée
fireworks le feu d'artifice
first premier
first aid les premiers soins (m)
first class première classe
first floor le premier étage
first name le prénom
fish le poisson
fishing la pêche; to go fishing
    aller à la pêche
fishing rod la canne à pêche
fishmonger's la poissonnerie
five cinq
fizzy water l'eau gazeuse (f)
flag le drapeau
flash (camera) le flash
flat (level) plat
flat tyre le pneu crevé
flavour le goût
flea la puce
flight le vol
flight attendant l'hôtesse
    de l'air (f)
flip-flops les tongs (f)
flippers les palmes (f)
floor (ground) le plancher;
    (storey) l'étage (m)
florist la fleuriste
flour la farine
flower la fleur
flowerbed le parterre
    de fleurs
flute la flûte
fly (insect) la mouche; (verb:
    of plane etc) voler; (of
    person) prendre l'avion
fog le brouillard
folk music la musique
    folklorique
food la nourriture
food poisoning l'intoxication
    alimentaire (f)
foot le pied
football le football
for pour; for me pour moi;
    what for? pour quoi faire?;
    for a week pour une
    semaine
foreigner l'étranger (m)
forest la forêt
forget oublier
fork la fourchette
fortnight quinze jours
forty quarante
fountain pen le stylo-plume
four quatre
fourteen quatorze
fourth quatrième
France la France

free (no cost) **gratuit**; (at liberty) **libre**
freezer **le congélateur**
French **français(e)**
Friday **vendredi**
fridge **le frigo**
fried **frit**
friend **l'ami(e)**
friendly **amical, gentil**
fringe **la frange**
front: in front **devant**
frost **le gel**
frozen foods **les produits surgelés** (m)
fruit **le fruit**
fruit juice **le jus de fruit**
fry **frire**
frying pan **la poêle**
full **complet**; *I'm full!* **j'ai l'estomac bien rempli!**
full board **la pension complète**
funny **drôle**
furnished **meublé**
furniture **les meubles** (m)

G

garage **le garage**
garden **le jardin**
garden centre **la jardinerie**
garlic **l'ail** (m)
gas **le gaz**
gas-permeable lenses **les lentilles semi-souples** (f)
gate **le portail, la grille**; (at airport) **la porte d'embarquement**
gay **homosexuel**
gear (car) **la vitesse**
gearbox **la boîte de vitesses**
gearstick **le levier de vitesse**
gel **le gel**
German **allemand(e)**
Germany **l'Allemagne** (f)
get (fetch) **aller chercher**; *have you got ...?* **avez-vous ...?**; *to get the train* **prendre le train**; *get back: we get back tomorrow* **nous rentrons demain**; *to get something back* **récupérer quelque chose**
get in **entrer**; (arrive) **arriver**
get off (bus etc) **descendre**
get on (bus etc) **monter**
get out **sortir**
get up **se lever**
gift **le cadeau**
gin **le gin**
ginger **le gingembre**

girl (child) **la fille**; (young woman) **la jeune fille**
girlfriend **la petite amie**
give **donner**
glad **heureux**
glass **le verre**
glasses **les lunettes** (f)
gloves **les gants** (m)
glue **la colle**
go **aller**
gold **l'or** (m)
golf **le golf**
golf course **le parcours de golf**
good **bon**, (fem) **bonne**; *good!* **bien!**
goodbye **au revoir**
good evening **bonsoir**
government **le gouvernement**
granddaughter **la petite-fille**
grandfather **le grand-père**
grandmother **la grand-mère**
grandparents **les grands-parents** (m)
grandson **le petit-fils**
grapes **les raisins** (m)
grass **l'herbe** (f)
Great Britain **la Grande-Bretagne**
green **vert**
grey **gris**
grill **le gril**
grilled **grillé(e)**
grocer's **l'épicerie** (f)
ground floor **le rez-de-chaussée**
groundsheet **le tapis de sol**
guarantee **la garantie**; (verb) **garantir**
guard (train) **le chef de train**
guest **l'invitée**
guide **le/la guide**
guide book **le guide**
guitar **la guitare**
gun (rifle) **le fusil**; (pistol) **le pistolet**
gutter **la gouttière**

H

hair **les cheveux** (m); *long/short hair* **les cheveux longs/courts**
haircut **la coupe (de cheveux)**
hairdresser **le coiffeur**
hairdryer **le sèche-cheveux**
hairspray **la laque**
half **demi**; *half an hour* **une demi-heure**

half board **la demi-pension**
ham **le jambon**
hamburger **le hamburger**
hammer **le marteau**
hamster **le hamster**
hand **la main**
hand luggage **le bagage à main**
handbag **le sac à main**
handbrake **le frein à main**
handkerchief **le mouchoir**
handle (door) **la poignée**
handsome **beau**
hangover **la gueule de bois**
happy **heureux**
harbour **le port**
hard **dur**; (difficult) **difficile**
hard lenses **les lentilles rigides** (f)
hardware shop **la quincaillerie**
hat **le chapeau**
have **avoir**; *have you got ...?* **avez-vous ...?**
hay fever **le rhume des foins**
he **il**
head **la tête**
head office **le siège social**
headache **le mal à la tête**
headlights **les phares** (m)
headphones **les écouteurs** (m)
hear **entendre**
hearing aid **l'appareil acoustique**
heart **le cœur**
heart condition **le problème au cœur**
hearts (cards) **cœurs**
heater **le radiateur**
heating **le chauffage**
heavy **lourd**
hedge **la haie**
heel **le talon**
hello **bonjour**
help **l'aide** (f); (verb) **aider**
hepatitis **l'hépatite** (f)
her: it's for her **c'est pour elle**; *give it to her* **donnez-le lui**
her: her book **son livre**; *her house* **sa maison**; *her shoes* **ses chaussures**; *it's hers* **c'est à elle**
hi **salut**
high **haut**
highway code **le code de la route**
hiking **la randonée**
hill **la colline**
him: it's for him **c'est**

pour lui;give it to him **donnez-le lui**

his: his book **son livre;** his house **sa maison;** his shoes **ses chaussures;** it's his **c'est à lui**

history **l'histoire** (f)

hitchhike **faire de l'autostop**

HIV positive **séropositif(ve)**

hobby **le passe-temps**

holiday **les vacances** (f)

home: at home (my home) **chez moi;** he's at home **il est chez lui**

homeopathy **homéopathie**

honest **honnête**

honey **le miel**

honeymoon **la lune de miel**

horn (car) **le klaxon;** (animal) **la corne**

horrible **horrible**

hospital **l'hôpital** (m)

host **l'hôte** (m)

hostess **l'hôtesse** (f)

hot **chaud**

hotel **l'hôtel** (m)

hour **l'heure** (f)

house **la maison**

household products **les produits entretien** (m)

hovercraft **l'aéroglisseur** (m)

hoverport **l'hoverport** (m)

how? **comment?**

how much? **combien?**

hundred **cent**

hungry: I'm hungry **j'ai faim**

hurry: I'm in a hurry **je suis pressé**

husband **le mari**

hydrofoil **l'hydrofoil** (m)

I

I **je**

ice **la glace**

ice cream **la glace**

ice rink **la patinoire**

ice skates **les patins à glace** (m)

ice-skating: to go ice-skating **aller patiner**

identification **la identification**

if **si**

ignition **l'allumage** (m)

ill **malade**

immediately **immédiatement**

impossible **impossible**

in **dans;** in France **en France**

indicator **le clignotant**

indigestion **l'indigestion** (f)

inexpensive **bon marché, pas cher**

infection **l'infection** (f)

information **l'information** (f)

injection **la piqûre**

injury **la blessure**

ink **l'encre** (f)

inn **l'auberge** (f)

inner tube **la chambre à air**

insect **l'insecte** (m)

insect repellent **la crème anti-insecte**

insomnia **l'insomnie** (f)

instant coffee **le café soluble**

insurance **l'assurance** (f)

interesting **intéressant**

internet **l'internet** (m)

interpret **interpréter**

interpreter **l'interprète** (m)

invitation **l'invitation** (f)

invoice **la facture**

Ireland **l'Irlande** (f)

Irish **irlandais(e)**

iron (for clothes) **le fer à repasser;** (verb) **repasser**

is: he/she is **il/elle est;** it is **c'est**

island **l'île** (f)

it **il; elle**

Italian **italien(ne)**

Italy **l'Italie** (f)

its **son; sa; ses** (see his)

J

jacket **la veste**

jam **la confiture**

January **janvier**

jazz **le jazz**

jeans **les jeans** (m)

jellyfish **la méduse**

jeweller's **la bijouterie**

job **le travail**

jog (verb) **faire du jogging;** to go for a jog **aller faire du jogging**

joke **la plaisanterie**

journey **le voyage**

July **juillet**

June **juin**

just: it's just arrived **ça vient juste d'arriver;** I've just one left **il ne m'en reste qu'un**

K

kettle **la bouilloire**

key **la clé**

keyboard **le clavier**

kidney **le rein**

kilo **le kilo**

kilometre **le kilomètre**

kind **gentil**

kitchen **la cuisine**

knee **le genou**

knife **le couteau**

knit **tricoter**

knitting needle **l'aiguille à tricoter** (f)

know (fact) **savoir;** (person) **connaître;** I don't know **je ne sais pas**

L

label **l'étiquette** (f)

lace **la dentelle;** (of shoe) **le lacet**

lake **le lac**

lamb **l'agneau** (m)

lamp **la lampe**

lampshade **l'abat-jour** (m)

land **la terre;** (verb) **atterrir**

language **la langue**

laptop **l'ordinateur portable** (m)

large **grand**

last (final) **dernier;** last week **la semaine dernière;** at last! **enfin!**

late **tard;** the bus is late **le bus est en retard**

later **plus tard**

laugh **rire**

launderette **la laverie automatique**

laundry (place) **la blanchisserie;** (clothes) **le linge**

law (subject) **le droit**

lawn **la pelouse**

lawn mower **la tondeuse à gazon**

lawyer **avocat(e)**

laxative **le laxatif**

lazy **paresseux**

lead **la laisse**

leaf **la feuille**

leaflet **le dépliant**

learn **apprendre**

leather **le cuir**

lecture theatre **l'amphithéâtre** (m)

leek **le poireaux**

left (not right) **la gauche**;
there's nothing left **il ne
reste plus rien**
leg **la jambe**
lemon **le citron**
lemonade **la limonade**
length **la longueur**
lens (camera) **l'objectif** (m)
less **moins**
lesson **la leçon**
letter **la lettre**
lettuce **la salade**
library **la bibliothèque**
licence **le permis**
life **la vie**
lift **l'ascenseur** (m)
light **la lumière**; (not heavy)
léger; (not dark) **clair**
light bulb **l'ampoule** (f)
lighter **le briquet**
lighter fluid **le gaz à
briquet**
light meter **la cellule
photoélectrique**
like (verb) **aimer**: *I like
swimming* **j'aime nager**; *I
don't like* **je n'aime pas**;
(similar to) **comme**
lime (fruit) **le citron vert**
lipstick **le rouge à lèvres**
liqueur **la liqueur**
list **la liste**
literature **la litérature**
litre **le litre**
litter **les ordures** (f)
little (small) **petit**; *it's a little
big* **c'est un peu trop
grand**; *just a little* **juste
un peu**
liver **le foie**
living room **le salon**
lobster **le homard**
lollipop **la sucette**
long **long**, (fem) **longue**
lost property **les objets
trouvés** (m)
loud **fort**; (colour) **criard**
love **l'amour** (m); (verb)
aimer
lover **l'amant** (m)
low **bas**
luck **la chance**; *good luck!*
bonne chance!
luggage **les bagages** (m)
luggage lockers **la consigne
automatique**
luggage rack **le
porte-bagages**
lunch **le déjeuner**
Luxembourg **le
Luxembourg**

M

mad **fou**, (fem) **folle**
magazine **la revue**
maid **la femme de
chambre**
main courses **les plats** (m)
make **faire**
make-up **le maquillage**
man **l'homme** (m)
manager **le directeur**;
le chef
many **beaucoup**; *not many*
pas beaucoup
map **la carte**; (town map)
le plan
March **mars**
margarine **la margarine**
market **le marché**
marmalade **la marmelade
d'oranges**
married **marié**
mascara **le mascara**
mass (church) **la messe**
mast **le mât**
match (light) **l'allumette** (f);
(sport) **le match**
material (cloth) **le tissu**
matter: it doesn't matter **ça
ne fait rien**
mattress **le matelas**
May **mai**
maybe **peut-être**
me: it's me **c'est moi**; *it's for
me* **c'est pour moi**; *give it
to me* **donnez-le-moi**
meal **le repas**
mean: what does this mean?
**qu'est-ce que cela
veut dire?**
meat **la viande**
mechanic **le mécanicien**,
le garagiste
medication **les médicaments**
(m)
medicine **le médicament**;
(subject) **le médicine**
Mediterranean **la
Méditerranée**
meeting **la réunion**
melon **le melon**
menu **la carte**; *set menu*
le menu
message **le message**
microwave **le micro-ondes**
middle **le milieu**
midnight **minuit**
milk **le lait**
mine: it's mine **c'est à moi**
mineral water **l'eau
minérale** (f)

minute **la minute**
mirror **le miroir**; (car)
le rétroviseur
Miss **Mademoiselle**
mistake **l'erreur** (f)
mobile phone **le téléphone
portable**
modem **le modem**
Monday **lundi**
money **l'argent** (m)
monitor (computer)
le moniteur
month **le mois**
monument **le monument**
moon **la lune**
moped **la mobylette**
more **plus**; *more or less*
plus ou moins
morning **le matin**; *in the
morning* **dans la
matinée**
mosquito **le moustique**
mother **la mère**
motorboat **le bateau
à moteur**
motorcycle **la moto**
motorway **l'autoroute** (f)
mountain **la montagne**
mountain bike **le vélo
tout terrain**
mouse **la souris**
mousse (hair) **la mousse**
moustache **la moustache**
mouth **la bouche**
move **bouger**; (house)
déménager; *don't move!*
ne bougez pas!
Mr **Monsieur**
Mrs **Madame**
mug **la tasse**
museum **le musée**
mushroom **le champignon**
music **la musique**
musical instrument
**l'instrument de
musique** (m)
musician **le musicien**
mussels **les moules** (f)
must: I must **je dois**
mustard **la moutarde**
my: my book **mon livre**; *my
house* **ma maison**; *my
shoes* **mes chaussures**

N

nail (metal) **le clou**; (finger)
l'ongle (m)
nail clippers **la pince
à ongles**
nailfile **la lime à ongles**

nail polish **le vernis à ongles**
name **le nom;** *what's your name* **comment vous appelez-vous?**
nappy **la couche**
narrow **étroit**
near: near the door **près de la porte**
necessary **nécessaire**
neck **le cou**
necklace **le collier**
need (verb) **avoir besoin de;** *I need ...* **j'ai besoin de ...;** *there's no need* **ce n'est pas nécessaire**
needle **l'aiguille** (f)
negative (photo) **le négatif**
neither: neither of them **ni l'un ni l'autre;** *neither ... nor ...* **ni ... ni ...**
nephew **le neveu**
never **jamais**
new **nouveau,** (fem) **nouvelle; neuf,** (fem) **neuve**
news **les nouvelles** (f); (television) **les informations** (f)
newsagent's **le tabac; le tabac-journaux**
newspaper **le journal**
next **prochain;** *next week* **la semaine prochaine;** *what next?* **et puis quoi?**
nice (place etc) **joli;** (person) **sympathique**
niece **la nièce**
night **la nuit**
nightclub **la boîte de nuit**
nightdress **la chemise de nuit**
nine **neuf**
nineteen **dix-neuf**
ninety **quatre-vingt-dix**
no (response) **non;** (not any) **aucun**
nobody **personne**
noisy **bruyant**
none **aucun**
noon **midday**
north **le nord**
nose **le nez**
not **pas;** *he's not ...* **il n'est pas ...**
notebook **le carnet**
notepad **le bloc notes**
nothing **rien**
novel **le roman**
November **novembre**

now **maintenant**
nowhere **nulle part**
nudist **le nudiste**
number (figure) **le numéro;** (amount) **le nombre**
number plate **la plaque d'immatriculation**
nurse **infirmier;** (fem) **infirmière**
nut (fruit) **la noix;** (for bolt) **l'écrou** (m)

O

oars **les rames** (f)
occasionally **de temps en temps**
October **octobre**
of **de**
of course **bien sûr**
office **le bureau**
often **souvent**
oil **l'huile** (f)
ointment **la pommade**
OK **d'accord**
old **vieux,** (fem) **vieille;** *how old are you?* **quel âge avez-vous?**
olive **l'olive** (f)
omelette **l'omelette** (f)
on ... **sur ...**
one **un/une**
onion **l'oignon** (m)
only **seulement**
open **ouvert** (adj); (verb) **ouvrir**
opening times **les heures d'ouverture** (f)
operating theatre **la salle d'opérations**
operation **l'opération** (f)
operator (phone) **l'opérateur** (m)
opposite **en face de**
optician's **l'opticien** (m)
or **ou**
orange (fruit) **l'orange** (f); (colour) **orange**
orange juice **le jus d'orange**
orchestra **l'orchestre** (m)
ordinary **habituel**
organ (music) **l'orgue** (m)
other: the other ... **l'autre ...**
our: our house **notre maison;** *our children* **nos enfants;** *it's ours* **c'est à nous**
out: he's out **il n'est pas là**
outside **dehors**
oven **le four**

over (above) **au-dessus de;** (more than) **plus de;** (finished) **fini;** *it's over the road* **c'est de l'autre côté de la rue;** *over there* **là-bas**
overtake (in a car) **doubler**
oyster **l'huître** (f)

P

pack of cards **le jeu de cartes**
package **le paquet;** (parcel) **le colis**
packet **le paquet**
padlock **le cadenas**
page **la page**
pain **la douleur**
paint **la peinture**
painting **la peinture**
pair **la paire**
palace **le palais**
pale **pâle, blême**
pancake **la crêpe**
paper **le papier;** (newspaper) **le journal**
paraffin **le pétrole**
parcel **le colis**
pardon? **pardon?**
parents **les parents** (m)
park **le jardin public;** (verb) **garer**
parting (in hair) **la raie**
party (celebration) **la fête, la soirée;** (group) **le groupe;** (political) **le parti**
passenger **le passager**
passport **le passeport**
passport control **le contrôle des passeports**
password **le mot de passe**
pasta **les pâtes** (f)
path **le chemin, l'allée** (f)
pavement **le trottoir**
pay **payer**
payment **le paiement**
peach **la pêche**
peanuts **les cacahuètes** (f)
pear **la poire**
pearl **la perle**
peas **les petits pois** (m)
pedestrian **le piéton**
peg **la pince à linge**
pen **le stylo**
pencil **le crayon**
pencil sharpener **le taille-crayon**
penknife **le canif**
pen pal **le correspondant**
people **les gens** (m)

pepper (and salt) **le poivre;** (red/green) **le poivron**

peppermints **les bonbons à la menthe** (m)

per: per night **par nuit**

perfect **parfait**

perfume **le parfum**

perhaps **peut-être**

perm **la permanente**

pet passport **le passeport d'animaux**

petrol **l'essence** (f)

petrol station **la station-service**

pets **les animaux (familiers)** (m)

phonecard **la carte téléphonique**

photocopier **le copieur**

photograph **la photo;** (verb) **photographier**

photographer **le/la photographe**

phrase book **le guide de conversation**

piano **le piano**

pickpocket **le pickpocket**

picnic **le pique-nique**

piece **le morceau**

pill **le comprimé**

pillow **l'oreiller** (m)

pilot **le pilote**

PIN **le code**

pin **l'épingle** (f)

pineapple **l'ananas** (m)

pink **rose**

pipe (for smoking) **la pipe;** (for water) **le tuyau**

piston **le piston**

pitch **l'emplacement** (m)

pizza **la pizza**

place **l'endroit** (m); *at your place* **chez vous**

plant **la plante**

plaster **le pansement**

plastic **le plastique**

plastic bag **le sac**

plastic wrap **le film alimentaire transparent**

plate **l'assiette** (f)

platform **le quai**

play (theatre) **la pièce;** (verb) **jouer**

please **s'il vous plaît**

pleased: pleased to meet you **enchanté(e)**

plug (electrical) **la prise;** (sink) **le bouchon**

plumber (occupation) **le plombier**

pocket **la poche**

poison **le poison**

police **la police**

police officer **le policier**

police report **le rapport de police**

police station **le commissariat**

politics **la politique**

poor **pauvre;** (bad quality) **mauvais**

pop music **la musique pop**

pork **le porc**

port (harbour) **le port;** (drink) **le porto**

porter **le porteur**

possible **possible**

post **la poste;** (verb) **poster**

postbox **la boîte à lettres**

postcard **la carte postale**

postcode **le code postal**

poster (outside) **l'affiche** (f); (inside) **le poster**

postman **le facteur**

post office **la poste**

potato **la pomme de terre**

poultry **la volaille**

pound (money, weight) **la livre**

powder **la poudre**

pram **le landau**

prefer **préférer**

prescription **l'ordonnance** (f)

pretty (beautiful) **joli;** (quite) **plutôt**

price **le prix**

priest **le prêtre**

printer **l'imprimante** (f)

private **privé**

problem **le problème**

profession **la profession**

professor **le professeur**

profits **les bénéfices** (m)

public **le public**

pull **tirer**

puncture **la crevaison**

purple **violet**

purse **le porte-monnaie**

push **pousser**

pushchair **la poussette**

put **mettre**

pyjamas **le pyjama**

Q

quality **la qualité**

quarter **le quart**

question **la question**

queue **la queue;** (verb) **faire la queue**

quick **rapide**

quiet (preson) **silencieux;** (street, etc) **tranquille**

quite (fairly) **assez;** (fully) **très**

R

rabbit **le lapin**

radiator **le radiateur**

radio **la radio**

radish **le radis**

rail: by rail **par chemin de fer**

railway **le chemin de fer**

rain **la pluie**

raincoat **l'imperméable** (m)

raisin **le raisin sec**

rake **le râteau**

rare (uncommon) **rare;** (steak) **saignant**

rash **la rougeur**

raspberry **la framboise**

rat **le rat**

razor blades **les lames de rasoir** (f)

read **lire**

reading lamp **la lampe de bureau;** (bedside) **la lampe de chevet**

ready **prêt**

ready meals **les plats préparés** (m)

receipt **le reçu**

reception **la réception**

receptionist **le/la receptionniste**

record (music) **le disque;** (sports etc) **le record**

record player **le tourne-disque**

record shop **le disquaire**

red **rouge;** (hair) **roux**

refreshments **les rafraîchissements** (m)

registered post **en recommandé**

relax **se détendre**

religion **la religion**

remember: I remember **je m'en souviens;** *I don't remember* **je ne me souviens pas**

rent (verb) **louer**

reservation **la réservation**

reserve (verb) **réserver**

rest (remainder) **le reste;** (verb: relax) **se reposer**

restaurant **le restaurant**

restaurant car **le wagon-restaurant**

return (come back) **revenir;** (give back) **rendre**

return ticket **l'aller retour** (m)

rice **le riz**

rich **riche**

right (correct) **juste;** (not left) **la droite**
ring (jewellery) **la bague**
ripe **mûr**
river **la rivière;** (big) **le fleuve**
road **la route;** (in town) **la rue**
roasted **rôti**
rock (stone) **le rocher;** (music) **le rock**
roll (bread) **le petit pain**
roof **le toit**
room **la chambre;** (space) **la place**
room service **le room service**
rope **la corde**
rose **la rose**
round (circular) **rond;** it's my round **c'est ma tournée**
roundabout **le rond-point**
row (verb) **ramer**
rowing boat **la barque**
rubber (material) **le caoutchouc**
rubbish **les ordures** (f); **les détritus** (m)
rubbish bin **la poubelle**
rug (mat) **la carpette;** (blanket) **la couverture**
rugby **le rugby**
ruins **les ruines** (f)
ruler **la règle**
rum **le rhum**
run (verb) **courir**
runway **la piste**

S

sad **triste**
safe (not in danger) **en sécurité;** (not dangerous) **sans danger**
safety pin **l'épingle de nourrice** (f)
sailing **la voile**
sailing boat **le voilier**
salad **la salade**
sale **la vente;** (at reduced prices) **les soldes** (f)
salmon **le saumon**
salt **le sel**
same: the same ... **le/la même ...;** the same again, please **la même chose, s'il vous plaît**
sand **le sable**
sandals **les sandales** (f)
sand dunes **les dunes** (f)
sandwich **le sandwich**

sanitary towels **les serviettes hygiéniques** (f)
Saturday **samedi**
sauce **la sauce**
saucer **la soucoupe**
saucepan **la casserole**
sauna **le sauna**
sausage **la saucisse**
say **dire;** what did you say?; **qu'avez-vous dit?;** how do you say ...? **comment dit-on ...?**
scarf **l'écharpe** (f); (head) **le foulard**
schedule **l'emploi du temps** (m)
school **l'école** (f)
science **la science**
scissors **les ciseaux** (m)
Scotland **l'Ecosse** (f)
screen **l'écran** (m)
screw **la vis**
screwdriver **le tournevis**
sea **la mer**
seafood **les fruits de mer** (m)
seat **la place**
seat belt **la ceinture de sécurité**
second (of time) **la seconde;** (in series) **deuxième**
second class **en seconde**
secretary **le/la secrétaire**
see **voir;** I can't see **je ne vois rien;** I see **je vois**
self-employed **à mon compte**
sell **vendre**
seminar **le séminaire**
send **envoyer**
separate **séparé** (adj); (verb) **séparer**
September **septembre**
serious **sérieux**
seven **sept**
seventeen **dix-sept**
seventy **soixante-dix**
several **plusieurs**
sew **coudre**
shampoo **le shampooing**
shave: to shave **se raser**
shaving foam **la mousse à raser**
shawl **le châle**
she **elle**
sheet **le drap**
shell **la coquille**
shellfish **les crustacés** (m)
ship **le bateau**
shirt **la chemise**
shoelaces **les lacets** (m)
shoemaker **la cordonnerie**
shoe polish **le cirage**

shoes **les chaussures** (f)
shop **le magasin**
shopkeeper **commerçant;** (fem) **commerçante**
shopping **les courses** (f); to go shopping **faire les courses**
short **court; petit**
shorts **le short**
shoulder **l'épaule** (f)
shower (bath) **la douche;** (rain) **l'averse** (f)
shower gel **le gel douche**
shrimp **la crevette**
shutter (camera) **l'obturateur** (m); (window) **le volet**
sick: I feel sick **j'ai envie de vomir;** to be sick (vomit) **vomir**
side (edge) **le bord**
sidelights **les feux de position** (m)
sightseeing **le tourisme**
silk **la soie**
silver (colour) **argenté;** (metal) **l'argent** (m)
simple **simple**
sing **chanter**
single (one) **seul;** (unmarried) **célibataire**
single room **la chambre pour une personne; la chambre simple**
single ticket **l'aller simple** (m)
sink **l'évier** (m)
sir **monsieur**
sister **la sœur**
six **six**
sixteen **seize**
sixty **soixante**
size **la taille**
skates **les patins à glace** (m)
ski **le ski;** (verb) **skier**
ski boots **les chaussures de ski** (f)
skid (verb) **déraper**
skiing: to go skiing **faire du ski**
ski lift **le remonte-pente**
skin cleanser **le démaquillant**
ski pole **le bâton de ski**
ski resort **la station de ski**
skirt **la jupe**
sky **le ciel**
sled **la luge**
sleep **le sommeil;** (verb) **dormir**
sleeper **le wagon-lit**
sleeping bag **le sac de couchage**
sleeping pill **le somnifère**

sleeve **la manche**
slip **le jupon**
slippers **les pantoufles** (f)
slow **lent**
small **petit**
smell **l'odeur** (f); (verb) **sentir**
smile **le sourire**; (verb) **sourire**
smoke **la fumée**; (verb) **fumer**
snack **le snack**
snow **la neige**
so **si**
soaking solution (for contact lenses) **la solution de trempage**
soap **le savon**
socks **les chaussettes** (f)
soft **mou**
soft lenses **les lentilles souples** (f)
soil **la terre**
somebody **quelqu'un**
somehow **d'une façon ou d'une autre**
something **quelque chose**
sometimes **quelquefois**
somewhere **quelque part**
son **le fils**
song **la chanson**
sorry (apology) **pardon**; *sorry?* (pardon?) **pardon?**; *I'm sorry* **je suis désolé**
soup **la soupe**
south **le sud**
souvenir **le souvenir**
spade (shovel) **la pelle**; (garden) **la bêche**
spades (cards) **pique**
Spain **l'Espagne** (f)
Spanish **espagnol**
spare parts **les pièces de rechange** (f)
spark plug **la bougie**
speak **parler**; *do you speak ...?* **parlez-vous ...?**; *I don't speak ...* **je ne parle pas ...**
speed **la vitesse**
speed limit **la limitation de vitesse**
spider **l'araignée** (f)
spinach **les épinards** (m)
spoon **la cuillère**
sport **le sport**
sports centre **le centre sportif**
spring (mechanical) **le ressort**; (season) **le printemps**
square (in town) **la place**; (adj: shape) **carré**

stadium **le stade**
staircase **l'escalier** (m)
stairs **les escaliers** (m)
stamp **le timbre**
stapler **l'agrafeuse** (f)
star **l'étoile** (f); (movie) **la vedette**
start (beginning) **le début**; (verb) **commencer**
starters **les entrées** (f)
statement **la déposition**
station **la gare**; (underground) **la station**
statue **la statue**
steak **le steak**
steal **voler**; *it's been stolen* **on l'a volé**
steamed **à la vapeur**
steamer **le bateau à vapeur**; (cooking) **le couscoussier**
steering wheel **le volant**
sting **la piqûre**; (verb) **piquer**
stockings **les bas** (m)
stomach **l'estomac** (m)
stomach ache **le mal de ventre, le mal à l'estomac**
stop (bus) **l'arrêt (de bus)** (m); (verb) **s'arrêter**
storm **la tempête**
straight on **tout droit**
strawberry **la fraise**
stream (small river) **le ruisseau**
street **la rue**
street musician **le musicien des rues**
string (cord) **la ficelle**; (guitar etc) **la corde**
strong (person, drink) **fort**; (material) **résistant**
student **l'étudiant** (m)
stupid **stupide**
suburbs **la banlieue**
sugar **le sucre**
suit **le costume**; *it suits you* **ça vous va bien**
suitcase **la valise**
summer **l'été** (m)
sun **le soleil**
sunbathe **se faire bronzer**
sunburn **le coup de soleil**
Sunday **dimanche**
sunglasses **les lunettes de soleil** (f)
sunny **ensoleillé**
sunshade **le parasol**
suntan **le bronzage**
suntan lotion **la lotion solaire**
supermarket **le supermarché**
supper **le souper**

supplement **le supplément**
suppository **le suppositoire**
sure **sûr**
surname **le nom de famille**
sweat **la transpiration**; (verb) **transpirer**
sweater **le pull**
sweatshirt **le sweat-shirt**
sweet (not sour) **sucré**; (confectionery) **le bonbon**
swim (verb) **nager**
swimming **la natation**; *to go swimming* **aller se baigner**
swimming pool **la piscine**
swimming trunks **le maillot de bain**
swimsuit **le maillot de bain**
Swiss **suisse(sse)**
switch **l'interrupteur** (m)
Switzerland **la Suisse**
synagogue **la synagogue**
syringe **la seringue**
syrup **le sirop**

T

table **la table**
tablet **le cachet**
take **prendre**
take away: to take away **à emporter**
takeoff **le décollage**
talcum powder **le talc**
talk **la conversation**; (verb) **parler**
tall **grand**
tampon **le tampon**
tangerine **la mandarine**
tap (water) **le robinet**
tapestry **la tapisserie**
taxi **le taxi**
tea **le thé**
teacher (secondary) **le professeur**
telephone **le téléphone**; (verb) **téléphoner**
telephone box **la cabine téléphonique**
television **la télévision**
temperature **la température**
ten **dix**
tennis **le tennis**
tent **la tente**
tent peg **le piquet de tente**
tent pole **le montant de tente**
terminal **le terminal**
terrace **la terrasse**
than **que**
thank (verb) **remercier**; *thank you* **merci**; *thanks* **merci**

that (that one) **ça**; *that bus* **ce bus**; *that man* **cet homme**; *that woman* **cette femme**; *what's that?* **qu'est-ce que c'est?**; *I think that the ...* **je pense que le ...**

the **le/la**; (plural) **les**

theatre **le théâtre**

their: *their room* **leur chambre**; *their books* **leurs livres**; *it's theirs* **c'est à eux**

them: *it's them* **ce sont eux/elles**; *it's for them* **c'est pour eux/elles**; *give it to them* **donnez-le-leur**

then **alors**; (after) **ensuite**

there **là**; *there is/are ...* **il y a ...**

these: *these things* **ces choses**; *these are mine* **ils sont à moi**

they **ils**; (fem) **elles**

thick **épais**

thief **le voleur**

thin **mince, maigre**

think **penser**; *I think so* **je pense que oui**; *I'll think about it* **je vais y penser**

third **troisième**

thirsty: *I'm thirsty* **j'ai soif**

thirteen **treize**

thirty **trente**

this (this one) **ceci**; *this bus* **ce bus**; *this man* **cet homme**; *this woman* **cette femme**; *what's this?* **qu'est-ce que c'est?**; *this is Mr ...* **je vous présente M. ...**

those: *those things* **ces choses-là**; *those are his* **ils sont à lui**

three **trois**

throat **la gorge**

throat pastilles **les pastilles pour la gorge** (f)

through **à travers**

thunderstorm **l'orage** (m)

Thursday **jeudi**

ticket **le billet**; (underground, bus) **le ticket**

ticket collector **le contrôleur**

ticket office **le guichet**

tide **la marée**

tie **la cravate**; (verb) **nouer**

tight **étroit**

tights **les collants** (m)

tiles, tiling **le carrelage**

time **l'heure** (f); *what's the time?* **quelle heure est-il?**

timetable (train, bus) **l'horaire** (f)

tip (money) **le pourboire**; (end) **le bout**

tired **fatigué**

tissues **mouchoirs**

to: *to England* **en Angleterre**; *to Paris* **à Paris**; *to the station* **à la gare**; *to the centre* **au centre**; *to the doctor* **chez le docteur**

toast **le pain grillé**

tobacco **le tabac**

toboggan **le toboggan**

today **aujourd'hui**

together **ensemble**

toilet paper **le papier hygiénique**

toilets **les toilettes** (f)

tomato **la tomate**

tomorrow **demain**; *see you tomorrow* **à demain**

tongue **la langue**

tonic **le tonic**

tonight **ce soir**

too (also) **aussi**; (excessively) **trop**

tooth **la dent**

toothache **le mal de dents**

toothbrush **la brosse à dents**

toothpaste **le dentifrice**

torch **la lampe de poche**

tour **la visite**

tourist **le/la touriste**

tourist office **le syndicat d'initiative**

towel **la serviette**

tower **la tour**

town **la ville**

town centre **le centre-ville**

town hall **l'hôtel de ville** (m); **la mairie**

toy **le jouet**

track suit **le survêtement**

tractor **le tracteur**

trade fair **la foire-exposition**

tradition **la tradition**

traffic **la circulation, le trafic**

traffic lights **les feux** (m)

trailer **la remorque**

train **le train**

trainee **le stagiaire**

trainers **les tennis** (m)

translate **traduire**

translator **le traducteur**

travel agency **l'agence de voyages** (f)

tray **le plateau**

tree **l'arbre** (m)

trolley **le chariot**

trousers **le pantalon**

truck **le camion**

true **vrai**

try **essayer**

Tuesday **mardi**

tunnel **le tunnel**

tweezers **la pince à épiler**

twelve **douze**

twenty **vingt**

two **deux**

tyre **le pneu**

U

ugly **laid**

umbrella **le parapluie**

uncle **l'oncle** (m)

under ... **sous ...**

underground **le métro**

underpants **le slip**

understand **comprendre**; *I understand* **je comprends**; *I don't understand* **je ne comprends pas**

underwear **les sous-vêtements** (f)

university **l'université** (f)

university lecturer **le maître de conférences**

unleaded **sans plomb**

until **jusqu'à**

unusual **inhabituel**

up **en haut**; (upward) **vers le haut**; *up there* **là-haut**

urgent **urgent**

us: *it's us* **c'est nous**; *it's for us* **c'est pour nous**; *give it to us* **donnez-le-nous**

use (verb) **utiliser**; *it's no use* **ça ne sert à rien**

useful **utile**

usual **habituel**

usually **d'habitude**

V

vacancy (room) **la chambre à louer**

vaccination **la vaccination**

vacuum cleaner **l'aspirateur** (m)

valley **la vallée**

valve **la soupape**

vanilla **la vanille**

vase **le vase**

VCR **le magnétoscope**

veal **le veau**

vegetables **les légumes** (m)

vegetarian (adj) **végétarien**

vehicle **le véhicule**

very **très**; *very much* **beaucoup**

vet **le vétérinaire**
video (film/tape) **la vidéo**
view **la vue**
viewfinder **le viseur**
villa **la villa**
village **le village**
vinegar **le vinaigre**
violin **le violon**
visit **la visite**; (verb: place) **visiter**; (person) **rendre visite**
visitor **le visiteur**
vitamin pill **le comprimé de vitamines**
vodka **la vodka**
voice **la voix**
voicemail **la messagerie téléphonique**

W

wait **attendre**; *wait!* **attendez!**
waiter **le serveur**; *waiter!* **garçon!**
waiting room **la salle d'attente**
waitress **la serveuse**; *waitress!* **Mademoiselle!**
Wales **le pays de Galles**
walk (verb) **marcher**; *to go for a walk* **aller se promener**
wall (inside) **la paroi**; (outside) **le mur**
wallet **le portefeuille**
want (verb) **vouloir**; *I would like* **je voudrais**
war **la guerre**
wardrobe **l'armoire** (f)
warm **chaud**
was: I was **j'étais**; *he was* **il était**; *she was* **elle était**; *it was* **il/elle était**
washer **la rondelle**
washing machine **la machine à laver**
washing powder **la lessive**
washing-up liquid **le produit pour la vaisselle**
wasp **la guêpe**
watch **la montre**; (verb) **regarder**

water **l'eau** (f)
waterfall **la chute d'eau**
water heater **le chauffe-eau**
wave **la vague**; (verb) **faire signe de la main**
wavy (hair) **ondulé**
we **nous**
weather **le temps**
Web site **le site web**
wedding **le mariage**
Wednesday **mercredi**
weeds **les mauvais herbes** (f)
week **la semaine**
welcome: you're welcome **je vous en prie**
Wellington boots **les boîtes en caoutchouc** (f)
were: we were **nous étions**; *you were* **vous étiez**; *they were* **ils/elles étaient**
west **l'ouest**
wet **mouillé**
what? **comment?**; *what is it?* **qu'est-ce que c'est?**
wheel **la roue**
wheelchair **le fauteuil roulant**; **la chaise roulante**
when? **quand?**
where? **où?**
whether **si**
which? **lequel?**
whisky **le whisky**
white **blanc**, (fem) **blanche**
who? **qui?**
why? **pourquoi?**
wide **large**
wife **la femme**
wind **le vent**
window **la fenêtre**
windscreen **le pare-brise**
wine **le vin**
wine list **la carte des vins**
wine merchant **le négociant en vins**
wing **l'aile** (f)
winter **l'hiver** (m)
with **avec**; *with pleasure* **avec plaisir**
withdraw (verb) **retirer**
without **sans**
witness **le témoin**

woman **la femme**
wood **le bois**
wool **la laine**
word **le mot**
work **le travail**; (verb) **travailler**; (machine etc) **fonctionner**
worktop **le plan de travail**
worse **pire**
worst **le pire**
wrapping paper **le papier d'emballage**; (for presents) **le papier cadeau**
wrench **la clé anglaise**
wrist **le poignet**
write (verb) **écrire**; *written by* **écrit par**
writing paper **le papier à lettres**
wrong **faux**, (fem) **fausse**

X, Y, Z

x-ray **radio**
x-ray departement **la salle de radiology**
year **l'an** (m); **l'année** (f)
yellow **jaune**
yes **oui**
yesterday **hier**
yet **déjà**; *not yet* **pas encore**
yoghurt **le yaourt**
you (singular informal) **tu**; (plural; singular formal) **vous**
young **jeune**
your (singular informal): *your book* **ton livre**; *your house* **ta maison**; *your shoes* **tes chaussures**; *it's yours* **c'est à toi**; (plural; singular formal): *your house* **votre maison**; *your shoes* **vos chaussures**; *it's yours* **c'est à vous**
youth hostel **l'auberge de jeunesse** (f)
zip **la fermeture éclair**
zoo **le zoo**

DICTIONARY
French to English

The gender of French nouns listed here is indicated by the abbreviations (m) and (f), for masculine and feminine. Plural nouns are indicated by (m pl) or (f pl). French adjectives (adj) vary according to the gender and number of the word they describe; the masculine form is shown here. In most cases, you add an **-e** to the masculine form to make it feminine. Certain endings use a different rule: masculine adjectives that end in **-x** adopt an **-se** ending in the feminine form, while those that end in **-ien** change to **-ienne**. Some feminine adjectives that do not follow these rules are shown here and follow the abbreviation (fem). For the plural form, a (silent) **-s** is usually added.

A

à: *at*: **à la poste** *at the post office*; **à trois heures** *at 3 o'clock*; **à côté de** *beside*; **à demain** *see you tomorrow*; **à emporter** *to take away*; **à travers** *through*
abat-jour (m) *lampshade*
abricot (m) *apricot*
accélérateur (m) *accelerator*
accident (m) *accident*
acheter *to buy*
adaptateur (m) *adaptor (voltage)*
addition (f) *bill*
adhésif (m) *adhesive*
adresse (f) *address*
adresse électronique (f) *email address*
aéroglisseur (m) *hovercraft*
aéroport (m) *airport*
affaire (f) *bargain*
affaires (f pl) *business*
affiche (f) *poster (outside)*
affreux *awful*
agence de voyages (f) *travel agency*
agenda (m) *diary*
agent (m) *agent*
agneau (m) *lamb*
agrafeuse (f) *stapler*
agrandissement (m) *enlargement*
aide (f) *help*
aider *to help*
aiguille (f) *needle*; **aiguille à tricoter** *knitting needle*
ail (m) *garlic*
aile (f) *wing*
ailleurs *somewhere else*

aimer *to like/love*; **j'aime nager** *I like swimming*; **je n'aime pas** *I don't like*
air (m) *air*
alcool (m) *alcohol*
Algérie (f) *Algeria*
algérien(ne) *Algerian*
allée (f) *path*
Allemagne (f) *Germany*
allemand(e) *German*
aller *to go*
aller chercher *to get (fetch)*
allergique *allergic*
aller patiner *to go ice-skating*
aller retour (m) *return ticket*
aller simple (m) *single ticket*
allez-vous en! *go away!*
allumage (m) *ignition*
allumette (f) *match (light)*
alors *well then*
Alpes: les Alpes (m pl) *Alps*
amant (m) *lover*
ambassade (f) *embassy*
ambulance (f) *ambulance*
amer *bitter*
américain(e) *American*
Amérique (f) *America*
ami(e) *friend*
amical *friendly*
amour (m) *love*
amphithéâtre (m) *lecture theatre*
ampoule (f) *blister; light bulb*
an (m) *year*
ananas (m) *pineapple*
Andorre *Andorra*
anglais(e) *English*

Angleterre (f) *England*
animaux (familiers) (m pl) *pets*
animé *busy (street)*
année (f) *year*
anniversaire (m) *birthday*
annuaire (m) *directory (telephone)*
antigel (m) *antifreeze*
antiseptique (m) *antiseptic*
août *August*
apéritif (m) *aperitif*
appareil acoustique (m) *hearing aid*
appareil-photo (m) *camera*
appartement (m) *apartment*
appât (m) *bait*
appétit (m) *appetite*
apprendre *to learn*
après *after*
après-midi (m) *afternoon*
après-rasage (m) *aftershave*
araignée (f) *spider*
arbre (m) *tree*
arbre à cames (m) *camshaft*
architecture (f) *architecture*
arête (f) *fishbone*
argent (m) *cash; money; silver (metal)*
argenté *silver (colour)*
armoire (f) *wardrobe*
arrêt de bus (m) *bus stop*
arrière (m) *back (not front)*
arrivée (f) *arrival*
arriver *to arrive*
art (m) *art*
artiste (m) *artist*
ascenseur (m) *lift*

aspirateur (m) *vacuum cleaner*
aspirine (f) *aspirin*
assez *enough; fairly*
assiette (f) *plate*
assurance (f) *insurance*
asthmatique *asthmatic*
attaché-case (m) *briefcase*
attendez! *wait!*
attendre *to wait*
attention! *careful!*
atterrir *to land*
attirant *attractive*
au: au café *at the café;* **au revoir** *goodbye*
auberge (f) *inn*
auberge de jeunesse (f) *youth hostel*
aucun *not any; none*
au-dessus de *over (above)*
aujourd'hui *today*
aussi *too (also)*
Australie (f) *Australia*
australien(ne) *Australian*
automatique *automatic*
automne (m) *autumn*
autoroute (f) *motorway*
autre: autre chose *something else*
avance (f) *advance*
avant *before*
avec *with;* **avec plaisir** *with pleasure*
averse (f) *shower (rain)*
aveugle *blind (cannot see)*
avion (m) *aircraft*
avocat (m) *avocado*
avocat(e) *lawyer*
avoir *to have*
avril *April*

B

bac (m) *ferry (small)*
bagages (m pl) *luggage; baggage;* **bagages à main** (m pl) *hand luggage*
baigner: aller se baigner *to go swimming*
bain (m) *bath*
balai (m) *broom*
balcon (m) *balcony*
balle (f) *ball (tennis etc)*
ballon (m) *ball (football etc)*
banane (f) *banana*
bandage (m) *bandage*
banlieue (f) *suburbs*

banque (f) *bank*
bar (m) *bar (place)*
barbe (f) *beard*
barbecue (m) *barbecue*
barque (f) *rowing boat*
bas (m) *stockings; low (adj);* **en bas** *down*
bateau (m) *boat; ship;* **bateau à moteur** (m) *motorboat;* **bateau à vapeur** (m) *steamer*
bâtiment (m) *building*
bâton de ski (m) *ski pole*
batterie (f) *battery (car)*
baume après-shampooing (m) *conditioner (hair)*
beau, (fem) **belle** *beautiful*
bébé (m) *baby*
bêche (f) *spade (garden)*
beige *beige*
beignet (m) *doughnut*
belge *Belgian*
Belgique: la Belgique *Belgium*
bénéfices (m pl) *profits*
béquilles (f pl) *crutches*
besoin: avoir besoin de *to need;* **j'ai besoin de ...** *I need ...*
beurre (m) *butter*
bibliothèque (f) *library*
bicyclette (f) *bicycle*
bien sûr *of course*
bien! *good!;* **ça vous va bien** *it suits you*
bière (f) *beer*
bijouterie (f) *jeweller's*
billet (m) *ticket; banknote*
biscuit (m) *biscuit*
blanc, (fem) **blanche** *white*
blanchisserie (f) *laundry (place)*
blême *pale*
blessure (f) *injury*
bleu (m) *bruise; blue (adj)*
bloc notes (m) *notepad*
blond (adj) *blond*
bœuf (m) *beef*
boire *to drink;* **vous voulez boire quelque chose?** *would you like something to drink?*
bois (m) *wood*
boisson (f) *drink*
boîte (f) *box;* **boîte à lettres** *postbox;* **boîte de chocolats** *box of chocolates;* **boîte de conserve** *can*

(vessel); **boîte de nuit** *nightclub;* **boîte de vitesses** *gearbox*
boîtes en caoutchouc (f pl) *Wellington boots*
bol (m) *bowl*
bon, (fem) **bonne** *good*
bonbon (m) *sweet (confectionery);* **bonbons à la menthe** (m pl) *peppermints*
bondé *crowded*
bonjour *hello*
bon marché *inexpensive; cheap*
bonne chance! *good luck!*
bonsoir *good evening*
bord (m) *side (edge)*
botte (f) *boot (footwear)*
bouche (f) *mouth*
boucherie (f) *butcher's*
bouchon (m) *plug (sink); cork*
boucles (f pl) *curls*
boucles d'oreille (f pl) *earrings*
bouger *to move;* **ne bougez pas!** *don't move!*
bougie (f) *spark plug; candle*
bouilli *boiled*
bouillir *to boil*
bouilloire (f) *kettle*
boulangerie (f) *bakery*
bout (m) *tip, end*
bouteille (f) *bottle*
bouton (m) *button;* **boutons de manchette** (m pl) *cuff links*
bracelet (m) *bracelet*
branche (f) *branch*
bras (m) *arm*
Bretagne: la Bretagne *Brittany*
bretelles (f pl) *braces (clothes)*
briquet (m) *lighter*
britannique *British*
broche (f) *brooch*
brochure (f) *brochure*
broderie (f) *embroidery*
bronzage (m) *suntan*
bronzer: se faire bronzer *to sunbathe*
brosse (f) *brush;* **brosse à dents** (f) *toothbrush*
brosser *to brush*
brouillard (m) *fog*
brûler *to burn*

brûlure (f) *burn*
Bruxelles *Brussels*
bruyant *noisy*
budget (m) *budget*
bunker (m) *bunker*
bureau (m) *desk; office*
bureau de location (m)
  box office
bus (m) *bus*

C

ça *that (that one)*
cabine téléphonique (f)
  telephone box
cacahuètes (f pl)
  peanuts
cachet (m) *tablet*
cadeau (m) *gift*
cadenas (m) *padlock*
cadre (m) *executive*
  (in company)
cafard (m) *cockroach*
café (m) *café; coffee;* **café**
  crème *white coffee;* **café**
  soluble *instant coffee*
cage (f) *cage*
caisse (f) *check-out*
  (supermarket)
calculette (f) *calculator*
cambriolage (m)
  burglary
caméscope (m) *camcorder*
camion (m) *truck*
campagne (f)
  countryside
camping-car (m)
  camper van
Canada (m) *Canada*
canadien(ne) *Canadian*
canal (m) *canal*
canif (m) *penknife*
canne à pêche (f)
  fishing rod
canoë (m) *canoe*
caoutchouc (m)
  rubber (material)
capot (m) *car bonnet*
capsule (f) *cap*
  (bottle)
caravane (f) *caravan*
carburateur (m)
  carburettor
carnet (m) *notebook;*
  carnet de chèques (m)
  chequebook
carotte (f) *carrot*
carpette (f) *rug (mat)*
carré *square (adj: shape)*
carreau *diamonds*
  (cards)

carrelage (m) *tiles, tiling*
carte (f) *menu; card; map;*
  carte bancaire *debit card;*
  carte de crédit *credit card;*
  carte d'embarquement
  boarding pass; **carte des**
  vins *wine list;* **carte de**
  visite *business card;* **carte**
  postale *postcard;* **carte**
  téléphonique *phonecard*
casquette (f) *cap (hat)*
cassé *broken*
casserole (f) *saucepan*
cassette (f) *cassette*
cassis (m) *blackcurrant*
cathédrale (f) *cathedral*
cave (f) *cellar*
ce (bus) *that (bus)*
ceci *this (this one)*
ceinture (f) *belt;* **ceinture**
  de sécurité *seat belt*
célibataire *single*
  (unmarried)
cellule photoélectrique (f)
  light meter
cendrier (m) *ashtray*
cent *hundred*
centre (m) *centre;* **centre**
  sportif (m) *sports centre*
centre-ville (m) *town*
  centre
cerise (f) *cherry*
certificat (m) *certificate*
ces (choses) *these (things)*
c'est *it's;* **c'est tout**
  that's all
cet (homme) *that (man)*
cette (femme) *that*
  (woman)
chaise (f) *chair*
châle (m) *shawl*
chambre (f) *bedroom;*
  chambre à louer *vacancy;*
  chambre pour deux
  personnes *double room;*
  chambre simple *single*
  room
chambre à air (f) *inner*
  tube
champ (m) *field (farming)*
champignon (m)
  mushroom
chance (f) *luck*
changer *to change (money);*
  se changer *to change*
  (clothes)
chanson (f) *song*
chanter *to sing*
chapeau (m) *hat*
chaque *each; every*
charcuterie (f) *delicatessen*

chargeur (m) *charger*
chariot (m) *trolley*
charpentier (m) *carpenter*
chat (m) *cat*
château (m) *castle*
chaud *hot; warm;* **j'ai chaud**
  I feel hot
chauffage (m) *heating;*
  chauffage central *central*
  heating
chauffe-eau (m) *boiler; water*
  heater
chaussettes (f pl) *socks*
chaussures (f pl) *shoes;*
  chaussures de ski
  (f pl) *ski boots*
chauve *bald*
chef (m) *manager;* **chef**
  d'orchestre *conductor*
  (orchestra); **chef de train**
  guard (train)
chemin (m) *path*
chemin de fer (m)
  railway
cheminée (f) *fireplace;*
  chimney
chemise (f) *shirt;* **chemise**
  de nuit *nightdress*
chemisier (m) *blouse*
chèque (m) *cheque*
cher *expensive;* **pas**
  cher *inexpensive*
cheveux (m pl) *hair;* **les**
  cheveux longs/courts *long/*
  short hair
cheville (f) *ankle*
chez *at home;* **chez**
  moi; *at my house;* **chez**
  vous *at your place*
chien (m) *dog*
chiffon à poussière (m)
  duster
chiffres (m pl) *figures*
chips (f pl) *crisps*
chocolat (m) *chocolate*
chou (m) *cabbage*
chou-fleur (m) *cauliflower*
chute d'eau (f) *waterfall*
ciel (m) *sky*
cigare (m) *cigar*
cigarette (f) *cigarette*
cimetière (m) *cemetery*
cinéma (m) *cinema*
cinq *five*
cinquante *fifty*
cintre (m) *coat hanger*
cirage (m) *shoe polish*
circulation (f) *traffic*
ciseaux (m pl) *scissors*
citron (m) *lemon;* **citron**
  vert *lime*

clair clear; light (not dark)

classe (f) class

clavier (m) keyboard

clé (f) key; **clé anglaise** (f) wrench

clignotant (m) indicator

climatisation (f) air conditioning

cloche (f) bell (church)

clou (m) nail (metal)

cocktail (m) cocktail party

code (m) PIN

code de la route (m) highway code

code postal (m) postcode

cœur (m) heart; **problème au cœur** heart condition;

cœurs (m pl) hearts (cards)

coffre (m) boot (car)

cognac (m) brandy

coiffeur (m) hairdresser; barber's

coin (m) corner

col (m) collar

colis (m) parcel

collants (m pl) tights

colle (f) glue

collection (f) collection (stamps etc)

collier (m) collar; necklace

colline (f) hill

combien? how much?; **combien ça coûte?** how much does it cost?

comme like (similar to)

commencer to start

comment? how?; **comment allez-vous?** how are you?; **comment est-ce que ça s'appelle?** what's it called?; **comment vous appelez-vous?** what's your name?

commerçant(e) shopkeeper

commissariat (m) police station

commode (f) chest of drawers

compagnie (f) company; **compagnie aérienne** airline

compartiment (m) compartment

complet full

compliqué complicated

comprendre to understand; **je comprends** I understand; **je ne comprends pas** I don't understand

comprimé (m) pill; **comprimé de vitamines** vitamin pill

comptable (m/f) accountant

compte: à mon compte self-employed

concert (m) concert

concierge (m/f) caretaker

concombre (m) cucumber

conducteur (m) driver

conduire to drive

conférence (f) conference

confiseur (m) confectioner

confiture (f) jam

congélateur (m) freezer

connaître to know (person)

consigne automatique (f) luggage lockers

constructeur (m) builder

consulat (m) consulate

consultant(e) consultant

contraceptif (m) contraceptive

contre against

contrôle des passeports (m) passport control

contrôleur (m) ticket collector

conversation (f) talk

copieur (m) photocopier

coquille (f) shell

corde (f) rope; string (guitar etc)

cordonnerie (f) shoemaker

corne (f) horn (animal)

corps (m) body

correspondant (m) pen pal

corse Corsican

Corse: la Corse Corsica

costume (m) suit

côtelette (f) chop (food)

coton (m) cotton; **coton hydrophile** cotton balls

cou (m) neck

couche (f) nappy; **couches à jeter** (f pl) disposable nappies

coude (m) elbow

coudre to sew

couette (f) duvet

couleur (f) colour

couloir (m) corridor

coup de soleil (m) sunburn

coupe (de cheveux) (f) haircut

couper to cut, chop

coupure (f) cut

courant (m) current

courgette (f) courgette

courir to run

courroie du ventilateur (f) fan belt

courses (f pl) shopping; to go shopping **faire les courses**

court short

couscoussier (m) steamer (cooking)

cousin (m) cousin

couteau (m) knife

coûter to cost

couverture (f) blanket; rug

crabe (m) crab

crampe (f) cramp

cravate (f) tie

crayon (m) pencil

crème (f) cream; **crème anti-insecte** (f) insect repellent cream

crêpe (f) pancake

crevaison (f) puncture

crevette (f) shrimp

crier to cry (shout)

croisière (f) cruise

crustacés (m) shellfish

cuillère(f) spoon

cuir (m) leather

cuire to bake

cuisine (f) kitchen

cuisinier (m) cook

cuisinière (f) cooker

curry (m) curry

D

d'accord OK

danger danger; **sans danger** safe

dans in

danse (f) dance

danser to dance

de of

début (m) start (beginning)

débutant(e) beginner

décapsuleur (m) bottle opener

décembre December

décollage (m) takeoff

décolorer to bleach

décorateur (m) decorator

dehors outside

déjà yet; already

déjeuner (m) lunch

delco (m) distributor (car)

demain tomorrow

démaquillant (m) skin cleanser

déménager to move house
demi half; **une demi-heure** half an hour
demi-pension (f) half board
dent (f) tooth
dentelle (f) lace
dentier (m) dentures
dentifrice (m) toothpaste
dentiste (m/f) dentist
déodorant (m) deodorant
départ (m) departures
département (f) department
dépliant (m) leaflet
déposition (f) statement
déraper skid (verb)
dernier last (final); **la semaine dernière** last week
derrière behind
descendre to get off (bus etc)
designer (m) designer
désolé: je suis désolé(e) I'm sorry
desserts (m pl) desserts
détritus (m) rubbish
deux two; **les deux** both
deuxième second (in series)
devant in front of
développer to develop
d'habitude usually
diabétique diabetic
diamant (m) diamond (jewel)
diarrhée (f) diarrhoea
dictionnaire (m) dictionary
diesel (m) diesel
différent different; **c'est différent** that's different
difficile difficult
dimanche Sunday
dîner (m) dinner
dire to say; **qu'avez-vous dit?** what did you say?; **comment dit-on ...?** how do you say ...?; **qu'est-ce que cela veut dire?** what does this mean?
directeur (m) director
discothèque (m) disco
disquaire (m) record shop
disque (m) record (music); **disque compact** (m) compact disc
distributeur automatique (m) cash machine

divertissement (m) entertainment
divorcé divorced
dix ten
dix-huit eighteen
dix-neuf nineteen
dix-sept seventeen
docteur (m) doctor
document (m) document
doigt (m) finger
dois: je dois ... I must ...
dollar (m) dollar
donner give
dormir to sleep
dos (m) back (body)
douane (f) customs
doubler to overtake (in a car)
douche (f) shower (bath)
douleur (f) ache; pain
douze twelve
drap (m) sheet
drapeau (m) flag
draps (m pl) bed linen
droit (m) law
droite right (not left)
drôle funny
dunes (f pl) sand dunes
dur hard

E

eau (f) water; **eau gazeuse** fizzy water; **eau minérale** mineral water; **eau potable** drinking water; **eau de Javel** bleach
échanger to exchange
écharpe (f) scarf
échecs (m pl) chess
école (f) school
Ecosse: l'Ecosse (f) Scotland
écouteurs (m) headphones
écran (m) screen
écrevisse (f) crayfish (freshwater)
écrire to write; **écrit par ...** written by ...
écrou (m) nut (for bolt)
église (f) church
élastique (m) elastic band; elastic (adj)
électricien(ne) electrician
électricité (f) electricity
électrique electric
elle she
elles they (fem)
email (m) email
embrayage (m) clutch
émeraude (f) emerald

emplacement (m) pitch
emploi du temps (m) schedule
en in; **en France** in France
enchanté(e) pleased to meet you
encore: encore un café another coffee
encre (f) ink
endormi asleep
endroit (m) place
enfant (m) child
enfin! at last!
ennuyeux boring
enregistrement (m) check-in; **enregistrement des bagages** baggage check-in
ensemble together
ensoleillé sunny
ensuite then (after)
entendre hear
entre ... between ...
entrée (f) entrance
entrées (f pl) starters
enveloppe (f) envelope
envie: j'ai envie de ... I feel like ...
environ about
envoyer to send
épais thick
épaule (f) shoulder
épicerie (f) grocer's
épileptique epileptic
épinards (m) spinach
épingle (f) pin; **épingle de nourrice** safety pin
erreur (f) mistake
escalier (m) stairs; staircase; **escalier roulant** escalator
Espagne: l'Espagne (f) Spain
espagnol Spanish
essayer to try
essence (f) petrol
essieu (m) axle
est (m) east
est is; **il/elle est** he/she is; **c'est** it is
estimation (f) estimate
estomac (m) stomach
et and
étage (m) floor (storey)
été (m) summer
étiquette (f) label
étoile (f) star
étouffant close (stuffy)
étranger (m) foreigner
étroit narrow; tight

étudiant (m) *student*
eux: c'est à eux *it's theirs;*
  c'est pour eux/elles *it's
  for them*
evanouir *to faint*
évier (m) *sink*
excédent de bagages (m)
  excess baggage
excellent *excellent*
excursion (f) *excursion*
exemple (m) *example*
exposition (f) *exhibition*
exprès *deliberately*
extérieure (f) *exterior;*
  exterior (adj)
  exterior **extincteur** (m)
  fire extinguisher

F

face: en face de *opposite*
facile *easy*
**façon: d'une façon ou
  d'une autre** *somehow*
facteur (m) *postman*
facture (f) *invoice*
faim: j'ai faim *I'm hungry*
faire *to do; make;*
  faire de autostop
  to hitchhike; **faire
  du jogging** *to jog;*
  **faire enregistrer ses
  bagages** *to check in;*
  faire la cuisine *to
  cook;* **faire la queue**
  to queue (verb);
  faire signe de la main
  to wave
fan (m/f) *fan* (enthusiast)
fantastique *fantastic*
farine (f) *flour*
fatigué *tired*
fauteuil (m) *armchair;*
  fauteuil roulant (m)
  wheelchair
faux, (fem) **fausse** *wrong*
félicitations! *congratulations!*
femme (f) *woman;
  wife;* **femme de chambre**
  maid; **femme de
  ménages** *cleaner*
fenêtre (f) *window*
fer à repasser (m) *iron*
  (for clothes)
ferme (f) *farm*
fermé *closed*
fermer *to close*
fermeture éclair (f) *zip*
fermier (m) *farmer*
ferry (m) *ferry* (large)
fête (f) *party* (celebration)

feu (m) *fire;* **feu d'artifice**
  fireworks; **feu de camp**
  campfire
feuille (f) *leaf*
feutre (m) *felt-tip pen*
feux (m pl) *lights; traffic lights;*
  feux de position (m pl)
  sidelights
fevrier *February*
fiancé *engaged* (couple)
fiancé(e) *fiancé(e)*
ficelle (f) *string* (cord)
fièvre (f) *fever*
figue (f) *fig*
fille (f) *girl; daughter*
film (m) *film*
fils (m) *son*
fin (f) *end*
fini *over* (finished)
flash (m) *flash* (camera)
fleur (f) *flower*
fleuriste (f) *florist*
fleuve (m) *river* (big)
flûte (f) *flute*
foie (m) *liver*
foire (f) *fair;*
  foire-exposition *trade
  fair*
foncé *dark;* **bleu foncé**
  dark blue
fonctionner *function*
  (machine, etc)
fond (m) *bottom*
football (m) *football*
forêt (f) *forest*
formulaire de demande
  (m) *application form*
fort *loud; strong* (person,
  drink)
fou, (fem) **folle** *mad*
foulard (m) *headscarf*
four (m) *oven*
fourchette (f) *fork*
frais, (fem) **fraîche** *cool*
fraise (f) *strawberry*
framboise (f) *raspberry*
français(e) *French*
France: la France *France*
frange (f) *fringe*
frein (m) *brake;* **frein à main**
  handbrake
freiner *to brake*
frère (m) *brother*
frigo (m) *fridge*
frire *to fry*
frit *fried*
frites (f pl) *chips*
froid (adj) *cold*
fromage (m) *cheese*
fromagerie (f) *cheese shop*
frontière (f) *border*

fruit (m) *fruit*
fruits de mer (m pl)
  seafood
fumée (f) *smoke*
fumer *to smoke*
fusil (m) *rifle*

G

galerie d'art (f) *art gallery*
gamelle (f) *animal's bowl*
gants (m pl) *gloves*
garage (m) *garage*
garagiste (m) *mechanic*
garantie (f) *guarantee*
garantir *to guarantee*
garçon (m) *boy;*
  garçon! *waiter!*
gare (f) *station;* **gare
  routière** (f) *bus station*
garer *to park*
garniture (f) *filling*
  (in sandwich, cake)
gâteau (m) *cake*
gauche *left* (not right)
gaz (m) *gas;* **gaz à briquet**
  (m) *lighter fluid*
gazoile (m) *diesel*
gel (m) *gel; frost;* **gel douche**
  (m) *shower gel*
gênant *embarrassing*
genou (m) *knee*
gens (m pl) *people*
gentil *friendly; kind*
gilet (m) *cardigan*
gin (m) *gin*
gingembre (m) *ginger*
glace (f) *ice; ice cream*
golf (m) *golf*
gomme (f) *eraser*
gorge (f) *throat*
goût (m) *flavour*
goutes (f pl) *drops*
gouttière (f) *gutter*
gouvernement (m)
  government
grand *big; large; tall;* **grand
  magasin** (m) *department
  store*
Grande-Bretagne (f)
  Great Britain
grand-mère (f)
  grandmother
grand-père (m) *grandfather*
grands-parents (m pl)
  grandparents
gras (m) *fat* (on
  meat, etc)
gratuit *free* (of charge)
grenier (m) *attic*
gril (m) *grill*

grillé(e) *grilled*
gris *grey*
gros, (fem) **grosse** (adj) *fat*
grotte (f) *cave*
groupe (m) *group; band* (musicians)
guêpe (f) *wasp*
guerre (f) *war*
gueule de bois (f) *hangover*
guichet (m) *cashier; ticket office*
guide (m) *guide; guide book;* **guide de conversation** (m) *phrase book*
guitare (f) *guitar*

H

habituel *ordinary; usual*
hache (f) *axe*
haie (f) *hedge*
hamburger (m) *hamburger*
hamster (m) *hamster*
handicapé *disabled*
haricots (m pl) *beans*
haut *high;* **en haut** *up;* **vers la haut** *upwards;* **là-haut** *up there*
hébergement (m) *accommodation*
hépatite (f) *hepatitis*
herbe (f) *grass*
heure (f) *hour; time*
heures d'ouverture (f pl) *opening times*
heureux *glad; happy*
hier *yesterday*
histoire (f) *history*
hiver (m) *winter*
homard (m) *lobster*
homéopathie *homeopathy*
homme (m) *man*
homosexuel *gay*
honnête *honest*
hôpital (m) *hospital*
horaire (f) *timetable* (train, bus)
horloge (f) *clock*
horrible *horrible*
hors-taxe *duty-free*
hôte (m) *host*
hôtel (m) *hotel*
hôtel de ville (m) *town hall*
hôtesse(f) *hostess;* **hôtesse de air** *flight attendant*
hoverport (m) *hoverport*
huile (f) *oil*
huit *eight*
huître (f) *oyster*
hydrofoil (m) *hydrofoil*

I

identification (f) *identification*
il *he; it* (m)
île (f) *island;* **les îles Anglo-Normandes** *Channel Islands*
ils *they* (m); **ils sont** *they are*
il y a … *there is/are …*
immédiatement *immediately*
imperméable (m) *raincoat*
impossible *impossible*
imprimante (f) *printer*
incendie (m) *fire* (blaze)
indigestion (f) *indigestion*
infection (f) *infection*
infirmier, (fem) **infirmière** *nurse*
information (f) *information*
informations (f pl) *news* (TV)
ingénierie (f) *engineering*
ingénieur (m) *engineer*
inhabituel *unusual*
insecte (m) *insect*
insomnie (f) *insomnia*
instrument de musique (m) *musical instrument*
intelligent *clever*
intéressant *interesting*
internet (m) *internet*
interprète (m) *interpreter*
interpréter *to interpret*
interrupteur (m) *switch*
intoxication alimentaire (f) *food poisoning*
invitation (f) *invitation*
invité(e) *guest*
irlandais(e) *Irish*
Irlande (f) *Ireland*
Italie (f) *Italy*
italien(ne) *Italian*
ivre *drunk*

J

jamais *never*
jambe (f) *leg;* **jambe cassée** (f) *broken leg*
jambon (m) *ham*
janvier *January*
jardin (m) *garden;* **jardin public** (m) *park*
jardinerie (f) *garden centre*
jaune *yellow*
jazz (m) *jazz*
je *I;* **je suis** *I am;* **je voudrais** *I would like*

jeans (m pl) *jeans*
jeu (m) *game:* **jeux vidéos** (m pl) *computer games*
jeu de cartes (m) *pack of cards*
jeudi *Thursday*
jeune *young*
joli *nice; pretty* (place etc)
jouer *to play*
jouet (m) *toy*
jour (m) *day*
journal (m) *newspaper*
joyeux anniversaire! *happy birthday!*
juillet *July*
juin *June*
jupe (f) *skirt*
jupon (m) *slip*
jus (m) *juice:* **jus d'orange** *orange juice;* **jus de fruit** (m) *fruit juice*
jusqu'à *until*
juste *right; fair* (correct); **ce n'est pas juste** *it's not fair*
juste un peu *just a little*

K, L

kilo (m) *kilo*
kilomètre (m) *kilometre*
klaxon (m) *horn* (car)
la *the* (fem)
là *there;* **il n'est pas là** *he's out*
là-bas *over there*
lac (m) *lake*
lacet (m) *shoelace*
laid *ugly*
laine(f) *wool*
laisse (f) *lead*
lait (m) *milk*
lames de rasoir (f pl) *razor blades*
lampe (f) *lamp;* **lampe de bureau** *reading lamp;* **lampe de chevet** *bedside lamp;* **lampe de poche** (f) *torch*
landau (m) *pram*
langouste (f) *crayfish* (saltwater)
langue (f) *language; tongue*
lapin (m) *rabbit*
laque (f) *hairspray*
large *wide*
lavabo (m) *basin* (sink)
laverie automatique (f) *launderette*
lave-vaisselle (m) *dishwasher*

laxatif (m) *laxative*
le *the* (m)
leçon (f) *lesson*
lecteur de cassettes (m) *cassette player*
léger *light* (not heavy)
légumes (m pl) *vegetables*
lent *slow*
lentilles *lenses* (f pl); **lentilles rigides** *hard lenses*; **lentilles semi-souples** *gas-permeable lenses*; **lentilles souples** *soft lenses*
lequel, (fem) laquelle: lequel? *which?*; **n'importe lequel** *either of them*
les *the* (plural)
lessive(f) *washing powder*
lettre (f) *letter*
leur: leur chambre *their room*; **leurs livres** *their books*
levée (f) *postal collection*
lever: se lever *to get up*
levier de vitesse (m) *gearstick*
librairie (f) *bookshop*
libre *free* (at liberty)
lime à ongles (f) *nailfile*
limitation de vitesse (f) *speed limit*
limonade (f) *lemonade*
linge (m) *laundry* (clothes)
lingettes (f pl) *baby wipes*
liqueur (f) *liqueur*
liquide: payer en liquide *to pay cash*
lire *to read*
liste (f) *list*
lit (m) *bed*; **lit d'enfant** (m) *cot*
littérature (f) *literature*
litre (m) *litre*
livraison (f) *delivery*
livre (m) *book*; *pound* (money, weight)
loin *far*
long, (fem) longue *long*
longueur (f) *length*
lotion solaire (f) *suntan lotion*
louer *to rent*
lourd *heavy*
luge (f) *sled*
lumière (f) *light*
lundi *Monday*
lune (f) *moon*; **lune de miel** *honeymoon*
lunettes (f pl) *glasses*;

lunettes de soleil *sunglasses*
Luxembourg (m) *Luxembourg*

M

ma: ma maison *my house*
machine à laver (f) *washing machine*
maçon (m) *bricklayer*
Madame *Mrs*
Mademoiselle! *waitress!*
magasin (m) *shop*; **magasin d'antiquités** *antique shop*
magnètoscope (m) *VCR*
mai *May*
maigre *thin*
maillot de bain (m) *swimsuit*; *swimming trunks*
main (f) *hand*
maintenant *now*
mairie (f) *town hall*
mais *but*
maison (f) *house*
maître de conférences (m) *university lecturer*
malade *ill*
mal à estomac (m) *stomach ache*
mal a la tête (m) *headache*
mal de dents (m) *toothache*
mal de ventre (m) *stomach ache*
manche (f) *sleeve*
Manche: la Manche *Channel*
mandarine (f) *tangerine*
manger *to eat*
manteau (m) *coat*
maquillage (m) *make-up*
marché (m) *market*
marcher *to walk*
mardi *Tuesday*
marée (f) *tide*
margarine (f) *margarine*
mari (m) *husband*
mariage (m) *wedding*
marié *married*
marmelade d'oranges (f) *marmalade*
marron *brown*
mars *March*
marteau (m) *hammer*
mascara (m) *mascara*
mât (m) *mast*
match (m) *match* (sport)
matelas (m) *mattress*;

matelas pneumatique *air mattress*
matin (m) *morning*
mauvais *bad*; *poor* (bad quality); **mauvais herbes** (f) *weeds*
mécanicien (m) *mechanic*
médecin (m) *doctor*
médicaments (m pl) *medication*
médicine (m) *medicine* (subject)
Méditerranée: la Méditerranée (f) *Mediterranean*
méduse (f) *jellyfish*
meilleur: le meilleur *the best*
melon (m) *melon*
même *same*; **le/la même ...** *the same ...*; **la même chose, s'il vous plaît** *the same again, please*
menu (m) *set menu*
mer (f) *sea*
merci *thank you*
mercredi *Wednesday*
mère (f) *mother*
mes: mes chaussures *my shoes*
message (m) *message*
messagerie (f): **messagerie électronique** *email*; **messagerie téléphonique** *voicemail*
messe (f) *mass* (church)
métro (m) *underground*
mettre *to put*
meublé *furnished*
meubles (m pl) *furniture*
micro-ondes (m) *microwave*
midday *noon*
miel (m) *honey*
mieux *better*
milieu (m) *middle*
mince *thin*
minuit *midnight*
minute (f) *minute*
miroir (m) *mirror*
mobylette (f) *moped*
mode (f) *fashion*
modem (m) *modem*
moi *me*; **c'est moi** *it's me*; **c'est pour moi** *it's for me*; **c'est à moi** *it's mine*
moins *less*
mois (m) *month*
mon: mon livre *my book*

moniteur (m) monitor (computer)

monnaie (f) change (money)

monsieur sir; Monsieur Mr

montagne (f) mountain

montant de tente (m) tent pole

monter to get on (bus etc)

montre (f) watch

monument (m) monument

morceau (m) piece

mordre to bite (dog)

morsure (f) bite (by dog)

mort dead

mot (m) word; mot de passe (m) password

moteur (m) engine (car)

moto (f) motorcycle

mou soft

mouche (f) fly (insect)

mouchoir (m) handkerchief

mouchoirs tissues

mouillé wet

moules (f pl) mussels

mourir to die

mousse (f) mousse (hair); mousse à raser (f) shaving foam

moustache (f) moustache

moustique (m) mosquito

moutarde (f) mustard

mur (m) wall (outside)

mûr ripe

mûre (f) blackberry

musée (m) museum; musée d'art art gallery

musicien (m) musician; musicien des rues street musician

musique (f) music; musique classique classical music; musique folklorique folk music; musique pop pop music

N

nager to swim

natation (f) swimming

navette (pour aéroport) (f) airport bus

né(e): je suis né(e) en ... I was born in ...

nécessaire necessary; ce n'est pas nécessaire that's not necessary

négatif (m) negative (photo)

négociant en vins (m) wine merchant

neige (f) snow

neuf nine

neuf, (fem) neuve new

neveu (m) nephew

nez (m) nose

ni: ni un ni autre neither of them; ni ... ni ... neither ... nor ...

nièce (f) niece

nier to deny

noir black

noix (f) nut (fruit)

nom (m) name; nom de famille (m) surname

nombre (m) number (amount)

non no

nord (m) north

nos: nos enfants our children

notre: notre maison our house

nouer to tie

nourriture (f) food

nous we; nous deux both of us; nous sommes we are; c'est à nous it's ours; c'est nous it's us; c'est pour nous it's for us

nouveau, (fem) nouvelle new; de nouveau again

nouvelles (f pl) news

novembre November

nudiste (m) nudist

nuit (f) night

nulle part nowhere

numéro (m) number (figure)

O

objectif (m) lens (camera)

objets trouvés (m pl) lost property

obturateur shutter (camera)

occupé busy (occupied)

octobre October

odeur (f) smell

œil (m) eye

œuf (m) egg

oignon (m) onion

oiseau (m) bird

olive (f) olive

omelette (f) omelette

oncle (m) uncle

ondulé wavy (hair)

ongle (m) nail (finger)

onze eleven

opérateur (m) operator (phone)

opération (f) operation

opticien (m) optician's

or (m) gold

orage (m) thunderstorm

orange (f) orange (fruit, colour)

orchestre (m) orchestra; stalls (theatre)

ordinateur (m) computer; ordinateur portable (m) laptop

ordonnance (f) prescription

ordre du jour (m) agenda

ordures (f pl) litter; rubbish

oreille (f) ear

oreiller (m) pillow

orgue (m) organ (music)

os (m) bone

ou or

où? where?

oublier to forget

ouest west

oui yes

ouvert (adj) open

ouvre-boîte (m) can opener

ouvrir to open

P

page (f) page

paiement (m) payment

pain (m) bread; pain grillé (m) toast

paire (f) pair

palais (m) palace

pâle pale

palmes (f pl) flippers

panier (m) basket

panne (f) breakdown (car); je suis tombé en panne I've had a breakdown

pansement (m) plaster

pantalon (m) trousers

pantoufles (f pl) slippers

papa dad

papier (m) paper; papier à lettres writing paper; papier cadeau gift wrap; papier d'emballage wrapping paper; papier filtre filter paper; papier hygiénique toilet paper

paquet (m) package, packet

par: par avion air mail; par chemin de fer by rail; par exemple for example; par nuit per night

parapluie (m) umbrella

parasol (m) sunshade

parce que because

parcours de golf (m) golf course

pardon!, pardon?
excuse me!; sorry! (apology);
pardon?
pare-brise (m) *windscreen*
pare-chocs (m) *bumper*
parents (m pl) *parents*
paresseux *lazy*
parfait *perfect*
parfum (m) *perfume*
parking (m) *car park*
parler *to speak, talk;*
parlez-vous ...? *do*
you speak ...?; ...
je ne parle pas ... *I don't*
speak
paroi (f) *wall (inside)*
parterre de fleurs (m)
flowerbed
parti (m) *party (political)*
particulièrement
especially
partout *everywhere*
pas *not;* **pas beaucoup** *not*
many; **pas encore** *not yet;*
il n'est pas ... *he's not ...*
passage (m) *driveway*
passager (m) *passenger*
passeport (m) *passport;*
passeport d'animaux (m)
pet passport
passe-temps (m) *hobby*
pastilles pour la gorge
(f pl) *throat pastilles*
pâtes (f pl) *pasta*
patinoire (f) *ice rink*
patins à glace (m pl) *ice*
skates
pâtisserie (f) *cake shop*
pauvre *poor (not rich)*
payer *to pay*
pays (m) *country (state);*
pays de Galles (m)
Wales
pêche (f) *peach; fishing:* **aller**
à la pêche *to go fishing*
peigne (m) *comb*
peigner *to comb*
peinture (f) *paint; painting*
pelle (f) *spade (shovel)*
pellicule couleur (f) *colour*
film
pelouse (f) *lawn*
pendant *during*
pendule (f) *clock*
penser *to think*
pension complète (f) *full*
board
père (m) *father*
perle (f) *pearl*
permanente (f) *perm*
permis (m) *licence;* **permis**

de conduire (m) *driving*
licence
personne *nobody*
petit *small*
petit ami (m) *boyfriend*
petit déjeuner (m)
breakfast
petite amie (f) *girlfriend*
petite-fille (f)
granddaughter
petit-fils (m) *grandson*
petits pois (m pl) *peas*
pétrole (m) *paraffin*
peut-être *maybe; perhaps*
phares (m pl) *headlights*
pharmacie (f) *chemist's*
photo (f) *photograph*
photographe (m/f)
photographer
photographier *to*
photograph
piano (m) *piano*
pickpocket (m) *pickpocket*
pièce (f) *coin; play*
(theatre)
pièces de rechange
(f pl) *spare parts*
pied (m) *foot*
piéton (m) *pedestrian*
pile (f) *battery (torch)*
pilote (m) *pilot*
pince (f): **pince à**
épiler *tweezers;* **pince**
à linge *peg;* **pince à**
ongles *nail clippers*
pinceau (m) *paintbrush*
pipe (f) *pipe*
(for smoking)
pique *spades (cards)*
pique-nique (m) *picnic*
piquer *to bite (snake), sting*
(insect)
piquet de tente (m)
tent peg
piqûre (f) *bite (snake);*
sting (insect); injection
pire *worse, worst*
piscine (f) *swimming pool*
piste (f) *runway; ski slope;*
piste pour débutants
beginners' slope
pistolet (m) *pistol*
piston (m) *piston*
pizza (f) *pizza*
placard (m) *cabinet*
place (f) *room (space); seat;*
square (in town)
plafond (m) *ceiling*
plage (f) *beach*
plaisanterie (f) *joke*
plan (m) *town map*

plancher (m) *floor*
(ground)
plan de travail (m)
worktop
plancher (m) *floor (ground)*
plante (f) *plant*
plaque d'immatriculation
(f) *number plate*
plastique (m) *plastic*
plat *flat (level)*
plateau (m) *tray*
plats (m pl) *main courses;*
plats préparés (m pl)
ready meals
pleurer *to cry (weep)*
plombage (m) *filling (in*
tooth)
plombier (m) *plumber*
plongeoir (m) *diving board*
plonger *to dive*
pluie (f) *rain*
plus *more:* **plus de** *more than;*
plus tard *later;* **plus ou**
moins *more or less*
plusieurs *several*
plutôt *quite*
pneu (m) *tyre;* **pneu crevé**
(m) *flat tyre*
poche (f) *pocket*
poêle (f) *frying pan*
poignée (f) *handle (door)*
poignet (m) *wrist*
poire (f) *pear*
poireaux (m) *leek*
poison (m) *poison*
poisson (m) *fish*
poissonnerie (f)
fishmonger's
poitrine (f) *chest*
poivre (m) *pepper (and*
salt)
poivron (m) *pepper*
(red/green)
police (f) *police*
policier (m) *police*
officer
politique (f) *politics*
pommade (f) *ointment*
pomme (f) *apple*
pomme de terre (f)
potato
pont (m) *bridge*

porc (m) *pork*
porcelaine (f) *china*
port (m) *harbour; port*
porte (f) *door (building);*
porte d'embarquement
(f) *gate (at airport)*
porte-bagages (m) *luggage*
rack

portefeuille (m) *wallet*
porte-monnaie (m) *purse*
porteur (m) *porter*
portière (f) *car door*
porto (m) *port (drink)*
possible *possible;* **dès que**
possible *as soon as possible*
poste (f) *post; post office*
poster (m) *poster (inside);*
(verb) *to post*
pot d'echappement (m)
exhaust (car)
poubelle (f) *rubbish bin*
poudre (f) *powder*
poulet (m) *chicken*
poupée (f) *doll*
pour *for;* **pour moi** *for me;*
pour une semaine *for a*
week
pourboire (m) *tip (money)*
pourquoi? *why?*
pousser *to push*
poussette (f) *pushchair*
pouvoir *to be able;* **je peux**
avoir ...? *can I have ...?;*
vous pouvez ...? *can*
you ...?
préférer *to prefer*
premier *first;* **premier**
étage (m) *first floor;*
première classe *first class;*
premiers soins (m pl)
first aid
prendre *to take;* **prendre le**
train *take the train;*
prendre un bain *have a*
bath
prénom (m) *first name*
près de *near;* **près de**
la porte *near the door;*
près de la fenêtre *by the*
window
préservatif (m) *condom*
presque *almost*
pressé: je suis pressé *I'm in*
a hurry
pressing (m) *dry cleaner's*
prêt *ready*
prêtre (m) *priest*
prie: je vous en prie *you're*
welcome
printemps (m) *spring*
(season)
prise (f) *plug (electrical);*
prise multiple *adaptor*
prise de sang (f) *blood test*
privé *private*
prix (m) *price;* **prix d'entrée**
admission charge; **prix du**
billet (m) *fare*
problème (m) *problem*

prochain *next;* **la semaine**
prochaine *next week*
produit pour la
vaisselle (m)
washing-up liquid
produits de beauté
(m pl) *cosmetics*
produits entretien
(m pl) *household products*
produits laitiers (m pl) *dairy*
products
produits surgelés
(m pl) *frozen foods*
professeur (m) *professor;*
teacher (secondary)
profession (f) *profession*
profond *deep*
promener: aller se
promener *to go for*
a walk
propre (adj) *clean*
prudent *careful;*
soyez prudent! *be*
careful!
public (m) *public*
puce (f) *flea*
pull (m) *sweater*
punaise (f) *drawing pin*
pyjama (m) *pyjamas*

Q

quai (m) *dock; platform*
qualité (f) *quality*
quand? *when?*
quarante *forty*
quart (m) *quarter*
quatorze *fourteen*
quatre *four*
quatre-vingt *eighty*
quatre-vingt-dix *ninety*
quatrième *fourth*
que *than*
quel âge avez-vous?
how old are you?
quelle heure est-il? *what's*
the time?
quelque chose *something*
quelque part *somewhere*
quelquefois *sometimes*
quelqu'un *somebody*
quelqu'un d'autre *someone*
else
qu'est-ce que c'est? *what's*
that?; what is it?
question (f) *question*
queue (f) *queue*
qui? *who?*
quincaillerie (f) *hardware shop*
quinze *fifteen;* **quinze jours**
fortnight

R

radiateur (m) *heater;*
radiator
radio (f) *x-ray; radio*
radis (m) *radish*
rafraîchissements
(m pl) *refreshments*
raie (f) *parting (in hair)*
raisin (m) *grape;* **raisin sec**
(m) *raisin*
rallonge (f) *extension lead*
ramer *to row*
rames (f pl) *oars*
randonée (f) *hiking*
rapide *fast; quick*
rapport de police (m) *police*
report
rare *rare (uncommon)*
raser: se raser *to shave*
rat (m) *rat*
râteau (m) *rake*
rayon (m) *aisle (supermarket)*
réception (f) *reception*
receptionniste (m/f)
receptionist
réclamation de bagages (f)
baggage claim
recommandé: en
recommandé *registered*
post
record (m) *record (sports etc)*
reçu (m) *receipt*
réduction (f) *discount*
regarde: cela ne vous
regarde pas *it's none of your*
business
regarder *to watch*
règle (f) *ruler*
rein (m) *kidney*
religion (f) *religion*
remercier *to thank*
remonte-pente (m) *ski lift*
remorque (f) *trailer*
rendez-vous (m)
appointment
rendre *to return (give back);*
rendre visite *visit (person)*
repas (m) *meal*
repasser *to iron*
réponder (m) *answering*
machine
reposer: se reposer *to rest*
(relax)
reseignments (m pl)
directory (telephone)
réservation (f) *reservation*
réserver *to book, reserve*
résistant *strong*
(material)
respirer *to breathe*

ressort (m) *spring* (mechanical)
restaurant (m) *restaurant*
reste (m) *rest* (remainder)
retard (m) *delay*
retirer *to withdraw*
rétroviseur (m) *car mirror*
réunion (f) *meeting*
réveil (m) *alarm clock*
revenir *to return* (come back)
revue (f) *magazine*
rez-de-chaussée (m) *ground floor*
rhum (m) *rum*
rhume (m) *cold* (illness); **rhume des foins** (m) *hay fever*
riche *rich*
rideau (m) *curtain*
rien *nothing*; **ça ne fait rien** *it doesn't matter*
rire *to laugh*
rivière (f) *river*
riz (m) *rice*
robe (f) *dress*
robinet (m) *tap* (water)
rocher (m) *rock* (stone)
rock (m) *rock* (music)
roman (m) *novel*
rond *round* (circular)
rondelle (f) *washer*
rond-point (m) *roundabout*
room service (m) *room service*
rose (f) *rose*; *pink* (adj)
rôti *roasted*
roue (f) *wheel*
rouge *red*; **rouge à lèvres** (m) *lipstick*
rougeur (f) *rash*
rouleaux (m pl) *curlers*
roux *red* (of hair)
rue (f) *street*
rugby (m) *rugby*
ruines (f pl) *ruins*
ruisseau (m) *stream* (small river)

S

sa: sa maison *his/her house*
sable (m) *sand*
sac (m) *bag*; **sac à dos** *backpack*; **sac à main** *handbag*; **sac de couchage** *sleeping bag*; **sac poubelle** *bin liner*
saignant *rare* (steak)
salade (f) *lettuce*; *salad*
salle (f) *room*; **salle à manger** *dining room*; **salle d'attente** *waiting*

room; **salle d'opérations** *operating theatre*; **salle de bains** *bathroom*; **salle de conférences** *conference room*; **salle de radiology** *x-ray departement*; **salle des urgences** *emergency departement*
salon (m) *living room*
salut *hi*
samedi *Saturday*
sandales (f pl) *sandals*
sandwich (m) *sandwich*
sang (m) *blood*
sans *without*; **sans plomb** *unleaded*
santé! *cheers!*
s'arrêter *to stop*
sauce (f) *sauce*
saucisse (f) *sausage*
saumon (m) *salmon*
sauna (m) *sauna*
savoir *to know* (fact); **je ne sais pas** *I don't know*
savon (m) *soap*
science (f) *science*
seau (m) *bucket*
sec, (fem) sèche *dry*
sèche-cheveux (m) *hairdryer*
seconde (f) *second* (of time)
seconde: en seconde *second class*
secrétaire (m/f) *secretary*
secteur (m) *field* (academic)
sécurité: en sécurité *safe* (not in danger)
seize *sixteen*
sel (m) *salt*
semaine (f) *week*
séminaire (m) *seminar*
sentir *to smell*
séparé (adj) *separate*
séparer *to separate*
sept *seven*
septembre *September*
sérieux *serious*
seringue (f) *syringe*
séropositif(ve) *HIV positive*
serveur (m) *waiter*
serveuse (f) *waitress*
service de pédiatrie (m) *children's ward*
serviette (f) *towel*
serviettes hygiéniques (f pl) *sanitary towels*
ses: ses chaussures *his/her shoes*
seul *alone*; *single* (one)

seulement *only*
shampooing (m) *shampoo*
short (m) *shorts*
si *if*; *whether*
SIDA *AIDS*
siège pour bébé (m) *car seat* (for a baby)
siège social (m) *head office*
silencieux *quiet* (person)
s'il vous plaît *please*
simple *simple*
sirop (m) *syrup*
site web (m) *web site*
six *six*
ski (m) *ski*; **faire du ski** *to go skiing*
skier *to ski*
slip (m) *underpants*
snack (m) *snack*
sœur(f) *sister*
soie (f) *silk*
soif: j'ai soif *I'm thirsty*
soir (m) *evening*; **ce soir** *tonight*
soirée (f) *party* (get together)
soit ... soit ... *either ... or ...*
soixante *sixty*
soixante-dix *seventy*
soldes (f pl) *sale* (at reduced prices)
soleil (m) *sun*
solution de trempage (f) *soaking solution* (for contact lenses)
sommeil (m) *sleep*
somnifère (m) *sleeping pill*
son livre *his/her book*
sonnette (f) *bell* (door)
sortie (f) *exit*
sortie de secours (f) *emergency exit*
sortir *to leave*
soucoupe (f) *saucer*
soûl *drunk*
soupape (f) *valve*
soupe (f) *soup*
souper (m) *supper*
sourcil (m) *eyebrow*
sourd *deaf*
sourire (m) *smile*; *smile* (verb)
souris (f) *mouse*
sous ... below ...; *under ...*
sous-sol (m) *basement*
sous-vêtements (f pl) *underwear*
soutien-gorge (m) *bra*
souvenir (m) *souvenir*; *remember* (verb); **je m'en**

souviens I remember; **je ne me souviens pas** I don't remember
souvent often
sport (m) sport
stade (m) stadium
stagiaire (m) trainee
station (f) underground station
station de ski (f) ski resort
station-service (f) petrol station
statue (f) statue
steak (m) steak
store (m) blind (window)
stupide stupid
stylo (m) pen; **stylo-bille** (m) ballpoint pen; **stylo-plume** (m) fountain pen
sucette (f) lollipop
sucre (m) sugar
sucré sweet (not sour)
sud (m) south
suisse(sse) Swiss
Suisse: la Suisse Switzerland
supermarché (m) supermarket
supplément (m) supplement
suppositoire (m) suppository
sur ... on ...
sûr sure
survêtement (m) track suit
sweat-shirt (m) sweatshirt
sympathique nice (person)
synagogue (f) synagogue
syndicat d'initiative (m) tourist office

T

ta: ta maison your house (singular informal)
tabac (m) tobacco; tobacconnist
table (f) table
tablette de chocolat (f) bar of chocolate
taille (f) size
taille-crayon (m) pencil sharpener
talc (m) talcum powder
talon (m) heel
tampon (m) tampon
tante (f) aunt
tapis (m) carpet; **tapis de sol** (m) groundsheet
tapisserie (f) tapestry
tard late; **bus est en retard** the bus is late
tasse (f) cup; mug

taux de change (m) exchange rate
taxi (m) taxi
télé cablée (f) cable TV
téléphérique (m) cable car
téléphone (m) telephone; **téléphone portable** (m) mobile phone
téléphoner to telephone (verb)
télévision (f) television
témoin (m) witness
température (f) temperature
tempête (f) storm; **tempête de neige** (f) blizzard
temps (m) weather; time; **de temps en temps** occasionally
tennis (m) tennis; **les tennis** (m pl) trainers
tente (f) tent
terminal (m) terminal
terrain de camping (m) campsite
terrasse (f) terrace
terre (f) land; soil
tes: tes chaussures your shoes (singular informal; plural noun)
tête (f) head
thé (m) tea
théâtre (m) theatre
ticket (m) ticket (underground, bus)
timbre (m) stamp
tire-bouchon (m) corkscrew
tirer to pull
tiroir (m) drawer
tissu (m) material
toboggan (m) toboggan
toi: c'est à toi it's yours
toilettes (f pl) toilets
toit (m) roof
tomate (f) tomato
ton: ton livre your book (singular informal)
tondeuse à gazon (f) lawn mower
tongs (f pl) flip-flops
tonic (m) tonic
torchon (m) dish cloth
tôt early
toucher to feel, touch
toujours always
tour (f) tower
tourism (m) sightseeing
touriste (m/f) tourist
tourne-disque (m) record player
tournevis (m) screwdriver

tous les deux both of them
tousser to cough
tout all; everything; **tout droit** straight on; **tout le monde** everyone; **tout seul** all alone
toux (f) cough
tracteur (m) tractor
tradition (f) tradition
traducteur (m) translator
traduire to translate
train (m) train
tranquille quiet (street, etc.)
transpiration (f) sweat
transpirer to sweat
travail (m) job; work
travailler to work
traverser to cross over
trèfle clubs (cards)
treize thirteen
trente thirty
très very
tricoter knit
triste sad
trois three
troisième third
trop too (excessively)
trottoir (m) pavement
tu you (singular informal); **tu es** you are
tunnel (m) tunnel; **le tunnel sous La Manche** Channel Tunnel
tuyau (m) pipe (for water)

U

un/une a; one; **un/une autre** another (different)
université (f) university
urgence (f) emergency
urgent urgent
utensiles de cuisine (f pl) cooking utensils
utile useful
utiliser to use

V

vacances (m pl) holiday
vaccination (f) vaccination
vague (f) wave; faint (adj)
valise (f) case
valise (f) suitcase
vallée (f) valley
vanille (f) vanilla
vapeur: à la vapeur steamed
vase (m) vase
veau (m) veal
végétarien (adj) vegetarian
véhicule (m) vehicle

vélo (m) *bicycle;* **vélo tout terrain** (m) *mountain bike*
vendre *to sell*
vendredi *Friday*
venir *to come;* **je viens de ...** *I come from ...*
vent (m) *wind*
vente (f) *sale* (transaction)
ventilateur (m) *fan* (ventilator)
vernis à ongles (m) *nail polish*
verre (m) *glass*
verres de contact (f pl) *contact lenses*
verrou (m) *bolt* (on door)
verrouiller *to bolt*
vert *green*
veste (f) *jacket*
vêtements (m pl) *clothes*
vétérinaire (m) *vet*
viande (f) *meat*
vide *empty*
vidéo (f) *video* (film/tape)
vie (f) *life*
vieux, (fem) **vieille** *old*
villa (f) *villa*
village (m) *village*
ville (f) *city; town*

vin (m) *wine*
vinaigre (m) *vinegar*
vingt *twenty*
violet *purple*
violon (m) *violin*
vis (f) *screw*
visage (m) *face*
viseur (m) *viewfinder*
visite (f) *tour; visit*
visiter *to visit* (place)
visiteur (m) *visitor*
vitesse (f) *gear* (car); *speed*
vodka (f) *vodka*
voile (f) *sailing*
voilier (m) *sailing boat*
voir *to see;* **je vois** *I see;* **je ne vois rien** *I can't see anything*
voiture (f) *car; train carriage*
voix(f) *voice*
vol (m) *flight*
volaille (f) *poultry*
volant (m) *steering wheel*
voler *to fly; steal;* **on a volé** *it's been stolen*
volet (m) *shutter* (window)
voleur (m) *thief*
vomir *to be sick* (vomit)
vos: vos chaussures *your*

shoes (singular formal; plural; plural noun)
votre: votre maison *your house* (singular formal; plural; singular noun)
vouloir *to want;* **je veux** *I want;* **vous voulez?** *do you want?*
vous *you* (singular formal; plural); **vous êtes** *you are*
voyage (m) *journey*
vrai *true*
vue (f) *view*

W, Y, Z

wagon-lit (m) *sleeper*
wagon-restaurant (m) *restaurant car*
whisky (m) *whisky*
yaourt (m) *yoghurt*
yeux (m pl) *eyes*
zoo (m) *zoo*

Acknowledgments

The publisher would like to thank the following for their help in the preparation of this book: Anne-Marie Miller for the organization of location photography in France; Hôtel-Restaurant, "Le Rabelais", Fontenay le Comte; Gare Routière de Fontenay le Comte; Pharmacie Parot, Nieul Sur L'Autise; Garage Gouband, Oulmes; Musée de l'Abbaye de Nieul Sur L'Autise (Cabinet Tetrac, Nantes); Boulangerie des familles, Coulon; Fromagerie, rue St Marthe, Niort; Fruits et Primeurs Benoit, Halles de Niort; Gare SNCF de Niort; Magnet Showroom, Enfield, MyHotel, London; Kathy Gammon; Juliette Meeus, and Harry.

Language content for Dorling Kindersley by **G-and-W publishing**
Managed by **Jane Wightwick**
Editing and additional input: **Pamela Wightwick, Christine Arthur, Leila Gaafar**

Additional design assistance: **Phil Gamble, Lee Riches, Fehmi Cömert, Sally Geeve**
Additional editorial assistance: **Kajal Mistry, Paul Docherty, Lynn Bresler**
Picture research: **Louise Thomas**

Picture credits

Key: t=top; b=bottom; l=left; r=right; c=centre; A=above; B=below

p2 Alamy: Ian Dagnall; *p3* DK Images: Peter Wilson: *p4/5* Alamy: f1 Online tl; images-of-france tr; Alamy: Andy Marshall bl; DK Images: br; Neil Lukas tcr; *p6/7* Laura Knox: cl; *p10/12* Alamy: BananaStock cAr; RubberBall cBl; Ingram Image Library: bl; *p12/13* Alamy: John Foxx cAr; RubberBall br; DK Images: cl; Steve Shott cBr; Ingram Image Library: tr, cr, *p14/15* Alamy: images-of-france tcr; Dreamstime.com: Slobodan Mraćina (cr); Ingram Image Library: cAl, cl, cBl, cAr, cBr, bcr; *p16/17* Alamy: RubberBall bcr; Ingram Image Library: tr; *p18/19* DK Images: David Murray tr; Ian O'Leary clB; *p22/23* DK Images: cl, Andy Crawford cAr; Susanna Price br; Magnus Rew tcrB; Ingram Image Library: bcl, tcr, *p24/25* DK Images: clA, Dave King tcr; *p26/27* Ingram Image Library: cl; *p28/29* DK Images: Andy Crawford tcr; Dave King cr; Matthew Ward bclA; Ingram Image Library: bcrA, bcr, *p30/31* Alamy: Comstock Images bcl; DK Images: cl, bclA; *34/35* Dreamstime.com: Slobodan Mraćina (cl); iStockphoto.com: nicolas_ (tcr); *p36/37* DK Images: bcl, bcr; Magnus Rew cl; Dreamstime.com: Slobodan Mraćina (cla); Ingram Image Library: bl; iStockphoto.com: nicolas_ (cr); *p38/39* Alamy: Imageshop / Zefa Visual Media cl; *p40/41* Alamy: images-of-france bl; Alamy: Justin Kase cAr; DK Images: cl, bcr; *p42/43* Alamy: Artografika Bildagentur cr; Alamy: Image Source tcr, cAr; Andy Marshall cAAr; *p44/45* Courtesy of Renault: c; *p46/47* Alamy: Artografika Bildagentur cr; images-of-france cl; Alamy: Imageshop / Zefa Visual Media br; DK Images: bcl; Ingram Image Library: trlB; Courtesy of Renault: tcr; *p48/49* Alamy: Agence Images tcr; Ian Dagnell cr; PCL bcr; Peter Titmuss cr; DK Images: bcl; *p50/51* Alamy: Robert Harding Picture Library c; *p52/53* Alamy: imagebroker tcr; Alamy: Image Farm Inc cAr; Photov.com / Hisham Ibrahim tcrB; DK Images: cl; *p54/55* Alamy: Frank Herholdt bcl; Jackson Smith cBl; Alamy: BananaStock cl; John Foxx c; Image Source cAr; ThinkStock tcr; DK Images: Andy Crawford bclA; *p56/57* Alamy: Agence Images clA; Ian Dagnell cl; PCL tl; Peter Titmuss cAl; DK Images: clAA; Courtesy of Renault: bc; *p58/59* Alamy: Michael Juno tcr; Alamy: Brand X Pictures cBl, cBBl; Image Source cAAl; DK Images: cAl; *p60/61* 123RF.com: shutswis (clb); Alamy: Robert Harding Picture Library bcr; Alamy: Image Source cAr; DK Images: Steve Gorton bl, tcrB; Pia Tryde cAAr; Ingram Image Library: cr; *p62/63* Alamy: Stephen Whitehorn c; *p64/65* Alamy: Arcaid bcrA; Alamy: GKPhotography cBr; Goodshoot cAAr; imagebroker c; Justin Kase tcrB; DK Images: Steve Tanner cAr; Ingram Image Library: tcr; *p66/67* Alamy: Arcaid tl; Alamy: Image Source cAr; DK Images: tr; Stephen Whitehorn bl; Ingram Image Library: br; *p68/69* Alamy: Balearic Pictures cr; f1 Online cBl; Doug Houghton cl; Indiapicture clB; Alamy: images-of-france clBr; Justin Kase bl; DK Images: Peter Wilson cAl; *p72/73* Alamy: imagebroker tcrB; Image Source cAr; Comstock Images tcr, Avery Weight-Tronix: bl; *p74/75* Alamy: Doug Norman bl; Ingram Image Library: c; *p76/77* Alamy: Balearic Pictures cBl; f1 Online cBl; Indiapicture bl; DK Images: Peter Wilson bcl; *p80/81* Getty: Taxi / Rob Melnychuk bc; Ingram Image Library: cAr; Xerox UK Ltd: tcr; *p82/83* Alamy: wildphotos.com tcr; Alamy: FogStock cAAl; Momentum Creative Group cAl; Shoosh / Up the Res cBl; Ingram Image Library: cl; *p84/85* Alamy: Brand X Pictures cr; f1 Online c; Alamy: BananaStock bl; SuperStock tr; Ingram Image Library: crB; *p86/87* Getty: Taxi / Rob Melnychuk tc; *p90/91* Alamy: Brand X Pictures tcr; DK Images: cl; David Jordan cAr; Stephen Oliver cr; Ingram Image Library: cBr; *p82/93* Alamy: Pixland cr; DK Images: cl; Guy Ryecart tr; *p94/95* Alamy: David Kamm cl; Phototake Inc bcl; Alamy: Comstock Images cr; ImageState Royalty Free bcr; DK Images: Stephen Oliver tcr; *p96/97* Alamy: Pixland br; DK Images: tl; Ingram Image Library: tr; *p98/99* Alamy: Bildagentur Franz Waldhaeusl bl; ThinkStock br; Dreamstime.com: Alexandre Dvihally (t); Getty RF: Photodisc Green c *p100/101* DK Images: Steve Gorton tcr; *p102/103* Alamy: The Garden Picture Library tcr; cAAr; Hortus b; D Hurst tcrB; Ingram Image Library: cAr, *p104/105* DK Images: Paul Bricknell cl(6); Jane Burton bcl; Geoff Dann cl(2); Max Gibbs cl(4); Frank Greenaway cl(3); Dave King cl(1), cAr, Tracy Morgan cl(5); *p106/107* Alamy: The Garden Picture Library br; DK Images: Peter Kinderlsey cr; *p110/111* Alamy: RubberBall cr; DK Images: Andy Crawford cl; *p112/113* Alamy: Image Source cl; DK Images: bl; Ingram Image Library: tcr; bcrA; *p114/115* Alamy: FogStock tcr; David R Frazier Photolibrary, Inc cBr; Alamy: Image Source cAr; Index Stock cAl; DK Images: Max Alexander cr; *p116/117* Alamy: The Garden Picture Library cAl; *p118/119* DK Images: Steve Gorton tcr; GettyNews: Giuseppe Cacace c; *p120/121* Alamy: ImageState / Pictor International cl; Alamy: Sarkis Images tcr; DK Images: cBl, bcl; Kevin Mallett br; *p122/123* Alamy: BananaStock cAr; Ingram Image Library: cl; *p124/125* Alamy: ImageState / Pictor International bclA; DK Images: cBl, bcl; Paul Bricknell tc(5); Geoff Dann tc(3); Max Gibbs tc(1); Frank Greenaway tc(2); Dave King tc(4); Kevin Mallett bl; Tracy Morgan tc(6); *p126/127* Alamy: imagebroker clB; Alamy: © Hisham Ibrahim / Photov.com blA; Image Farm Inc bl; *p128* DK Images: Neil Mersh.

All other images **Mike Good**.